# The  Ignited The Great War and The Cold War Sniper
## Ferdinand and Kennedy

By John S. Craig

*The Black Hand That Ignited The Great War and the Cold War Sniper – Ferdinand and Kennedy*

©Copyright John S. Craig, 2021

First Edition

Blurb Books

All images public domain /Cover images, Archduke Ferdinand and wife Sophie in Graef and Stift open touring car, Sarajevo, June 28, 1914; President Kennedy and wife Jacqueline in Lincoln Continental limousine, Dallas, Texas U.S.A. November 22, 1963; JFK limousine image Wikimedia.com

## Table of Contents

*Chapter 1. The Black Hand That Ignited The Great War* ............................................. *6*

*Chapter 2. The Assassination of JFK* ........ *82*

*About the Author* ................................... *188*

# Chapter 1. The Black Hand That Ignited The Great War

GAVRILO PRINCIP

"I am a Yugoslav nationalist, aiming for the unification of all Yugoslavs, and I do not care what form of state, but it must be freed from Austria." – Gavrilo Princip

Princip

7

In the dark of early morning June 11, 1903, Captain Dragutin Dimitrijevic, a large, muscular, twenty-six-year-old man known to his associates as "The Bull," or "Apis,"[1] lay on the floor of King Alexander Obrenovic's Belgrade palace. The palace guard had shot the Serbian Army captain three times, but not before Apis and his companions had slaughtered both the Serbian king and his queen. Apis eventually recovered from his wounds and a few years later would help form and guide a secret society of assassins: *Crna Ruka* (The Black Hand).[2] The Black Hand, founded in Belgrade, Serbia, in 1911 with the aim of uniting all Serbs, would drastically change European history. Apis empowered the Black Hand by recruiting young men infected with tuberculosis. The disease was so debilitating that Apis was able to enlist the afflicted on the notion that their only genuine chance to leave their mark would be to change Serbian history through the assassination of Serbia's enemies. One of these pathetic tuberculins was the Bosnia-born Gavrilo Princip, a teenager whose assassination of the Austria-Hungarian heir apparent, Archduke Franz Ferdinand, would help trigger the nightmare of the Great War, World War I, the War to End all Wars.

THE BALKANS

The "Balkans," Turkish for "mountains," refers to the people of the Balkan Peninsula, a portion of land in the southeast corner of Europe. The borders and names of the countries in this area have changed numerous times; it is a kaleidoscope of peoples of different racial and religious backgrounds at a critical juncture between the Muslims, Orthodox Christian and Catholic worlds. The Balkan Peninsula is home of Slovenia, Croatia, Bosnia-Herzegovina, Albania, Yugoslavia, Bulgaria, Turkey, Macedonia, and Greece;[3] it is bounded by the lower Danube River and the Black, Aegean, Mediterranean, Ionian, and Adriatic seas. The Balkan Peninsula is militarily significant because it links Europe and Asia. Six empires — Persian, Roman, Byzantine, Ottoman, Hapsburg, and Russian — have gone to great lengths to control the region and all paid greatly. In the Balkans, wrote C. L. Sulzberger, lived "sprightly people who ate peppered foods, drank strong liquors, wore flamboyant clothes, loved and murdered easily and had a splendid talent for starting wars . . . less imaginative westerners looked down on them with secret envy, sniffing at their royalty, scoffing at their pretensions, and fearing their savage terrorists."[4]

Philosophical and literary brilliance associated with this land, the land of Homer, Socrates, Aristotle, Aeschylus and countless others, as well as the twentieth-century genius scientist, the Croatia-born Nikola Tesla.[5] There are also many names legendary with mystery and might: the Pythia of the Oracle of Delphi,[6] the priestesses of Apollo who passed on messages from the gods to the mortals for a thousand years; Philip of Macedon, the Macedonian king who conquered most of Greece; Philip's son, Alexander the Great, the Macedonian who conquered the known world in his quest to spread the virtues of Hellenistic culture and take revenge for earlier Persian assaults; Spartacus, the leader of the Greek slave revolt against Rome;[7] Vlad Tepes (Vlad the Impaler), the Romanian leader whose ruthless tactics in fighting off the Turks fueled the legends that gave rise to the fictional vampire Dracula; Gavrilo Princip, the nineteen-year-old Bosnian assassin whose alliance with a secret society helped tip Europe into a cataclysmic war; Josip Broz, the Croatian-Slovenian Communist known as Tito, who helped lead the anti-Nazi resistance and fended off Soviet dominance, becoming President of a sovereign Yugoslavia that was known for its highly liberal version of market socialism; Slobodan Milosevic, the pro-Serbian Yugoslavian president associated with the Balkan Wars of the 1990s.

    The Ancient Greeks considered their contemporary Macedonians barbaric northerners with a strange and mysterious culture. Even the Macedonian language is largely a mystery, today, though it may have been a Greek dialect; not a single sentence of the original language has been retained.[8] As historian Eugene Borza put it, neither the Greeks nor the Macedonians considered the Macedonians to be Greeks. Although the Macedonians protected their southern neighbors from any possible invading Europeans, they were never accorded respect. However, Philip of Macedon's victory at the

Battle of Chaeronea in 338 BC made the Macedonians the true rulers of Greece and established the beginning of the Macedonian era. After Philip gained control of Greece, he turned his attention to conquering the Greek's long-time nemesis, the Persians, but his plans were cut short when he was assassinated.

Philip's twenty-one-year-old son, Alexander III of Macedonia (also known as Alexander the Great, Alexander Magnus), claimed the throne. Whether Philip's death was the result of a conspiracy or a lone assassin has been a matter of speculation for centuries. In some versions three men were part of the assassination. Athenians, Persians, or his ex-wife Olympia, so some say, commissioned the plot. Alexander executed his uncle, stepmother, and her immediate family, blaming them and others for his father's murder. This act summarily completed any investigation into the assassination and surely discouraged any other possible conspirators from questioning Alexander's claim to the throne.[9] Alexander took his father's conquest of Persia to heart and his sensational military victories spread Greek culture through northern Africa, southwestern Asia, Egypt, Libya, Iraq, Iran, Afghanistan, Pakistan, and other regions. Alexander's military campaign created the Hellenistic era (323-BC to 31 BC, 300 years of dominance that ended only during the rule of Rome's Augustus in 31 BC). Alexander's campaign created Alexandria, Egypt, with its great library and museum,[10] and marked the beginning of an international culture by actively exporting Greek achievements. Alexander was eventually revered by the Greeks as a conquering hero and is hated to this day by many of the ancestors of his victims; the source of his ambition has been the wonder of historians for centuries.[11] Inspired by heroic tales of the ancient and legendary Greek-Trojan War, he attacked Persian armies in particular, fearing their expansion would eventually sweep into the Balkan Peninsula.

Throughout the centuries Macedonia, which lies in the heart of the Balkan Peninsula, has been the claim of Greeks, Bulgarians, Serbs, Albanians, and Turks, all of whom believe that their ancestors' arrival in that land gives them the right to rule it. The Bulgars go so far as to claim there is no

Macedonia — it is only Western Bulgaria, a claim they back with the fact that 80% of the population speaks Bulgarian. Macedonia's fate is the fate of other Balkan nations: a struggle to exist as an autonomous nation but the victim of seemingly endless assaults by neighbors who believe the land to be rightfully theirs.

## ZOROASTER, JUDAISM, CHRIST, AND MOHAMMED

Zoroaster, a man born in the later part of the sixth century BC, in what is now Iran, claimed to be the spokesman of the one true God, Ahura Mazdah. Zoroastrianism is based on belief in a constant universal battle between good and bad spirits, the coming of the kingdom of God, a savior, and bodily resurrection, all concepts that have been recognized as a great influence on the framing of Judaism, Christianity, and Islam. Zoroastrianism was the principal religion in Persia for approximately one thousand years.

In the early fourth century, Roman Emperor Constantine the Great expanded the Roman Empire and the Christian Church by founding "New Rome," Constantinople. This expansion was an act that would have a profound impact on the future of the Balkans and subsequently the Western world. Constantine was inspired by a vision that assured him he would be successful in his conquests by employing the Greek monogram of Christ, the *Chi-Rho*. He marked the shields of his soldiers with the sign and was convinced of its divine power when he won a battle against his rival Maxentius at the Milvian Bridge crossing the Tiber.[12]

One of the most important battles in Roman history occurred on ancient Macedonian soil (known at the time as Thrace), when the barbarian Goths defeated a Constantinople-based Roman army at the Battle of Adrianople in AD 378. The battle, a mere 150 miles from Constantinople, was the precursor to the sacking of Rome in AD 410 by the Goths. The Goths' victory created more chaos for the Balkan region. In 380 the Roman Emperor Theodosius, the first Roman emperor nurtured in a Christian home, decreed through the Theodosian Code that all of his subjects would be Christians. Under his rule pagan temples were destroyed and "heathens" were persecuted. With the death of Theodosius in 395, the empire was split[13] with Rome centered in the West and Constantinople the East; the line of division in Europe ran south along the Drina River in the Balkans. Croatia and Bosnia lay to its west and modern Serbia[14] and Macedonia to its east. As the ancestors of the modern Slavs moved into this region in the sixth century from northern Europe and the Ukraine, they adopted either what came to be known as the Roman Catholic Church or the Eastern Orthodox (Byzantine) Church.

The birth of Mohammed[15] in 570 in Mecca would lead to the creation of the religion of Islam. Islam replaced Zoroastrianism as the predominant religion in Persia and quickly spread into other parts of the world to become one of the most widely followed religions of all time. Though Christians and Jews were required to pay large taxes and wear identifying clothing when they came under the rule of conquering Muslims, they were allowed to keep their religions; and Islam spread quickly into the Balkans.

The current three great religions of the world, Judaism, Christianity and Islam, have curious similarities and differences. All three share a linear view of time; recognize Abraham as a forefather of faith; believer in a messiah, resurrection of the body, the eventual destruction of the present world, a place of eternal torment for the wicked, levels of reward for the righteous, and the possibility through good works of eternal life. Some of the key differences of the religions that have caused so much tension are whether man is good, bad, or depraved; a place of purgatory; whether salvation is possible; whether the messiah has come or will come again; and how and when the world will be destroyed and reborn.[16]

Two Salonika-born monks (Cyril and Methodius) are credited with introducing Christianity to the Slavs of the Balkans in the late eighth century. They developed a Slavic script, called Glagolithic; this form of writing eventually was called Cyrillic and in various forms is still used by Serbs, Bulgarians, and Russians. This created another basic difference between the two Christian camps: the West using Latin and the East using Cyrillic. The Croatians were subject to the influence of Latin missionaries between the sixth and eighth centuries, an effort that kept

Western Catholicism strong for centuries in Croatia. With the final split of the Christian church in 1054 the seeds of dissent between the various ethnic groups were sown.[17]

Partly in an effort to unite the Christian empire fractured between a Rome-centered, Latin-based Catholicism and a Constantinople-centered, Cyrillic-based Eastern Orthodoxy, Pope Urban encouraged Christian crusaders to "recapture" the Holy Land, which resulted in decades of conflict (1096-1291) between Christian invaders and people who lay in their path to Jerusalem via Constantinople. The Crusaders entered Jerusalem in 1099 and slaughtered 40,000 Jewish and Muslim inhabitants, people who had lived together in peace for 460 years. The massacre was similar to the Roman invasion of Jerusalem in the first century. Subsequent waves of Crusaders succeeded in temporarily holding Jerusalem for Christianity. Violence was the rule, but Richard the Lionhearted tried European diplomacy when he suggested that his sister Joanna be married to the Sultan Saladin's brother al-Adil, creating a Christian-Muslim alliance that could rule Jerusalem in peace.[18] Everyone but Richard considered the

offer to be utterly bizarre. Saladin took back
Jerusalem for Islam in 1187. It has been said
that the three religions have eyed each other
with distrust ever since. [19]

## THE KARADJORDJE AND OBRENOVIC DYNASTIES

In the fourteenth and fifteenth
centuries, Turkish Muslim armies invaded the
Balkans, conquering Turnovo, Bulgaria in
1393, Serbia in 1441, Constantinople in 1453,
Bosnia in 1463, the Albanian fortress town of
Kruje in 1478, and Moldavia and Walachia of
Romania in 1501. By the sixteenth century the
Balkan countries were a mélange of religions
grounded in conflicting dogmas. The
indigenous ethnic groups were at war with
each other as well as with the despised
invading Turks of the Ottoman Empire.

In 1689, Arsenje Carnojevic, a
spiritual leader whom Serbs considered their
Patriarch, led the Serbs against the Turks and
encouraged them to aid the Austrian army.
On New Year's Day, 1690, the Turks crushed
the Austrians and the Serbs. Carnojevic,
fearing reprisals from the vengeful Turks, led
thousands of refugees away from the heart of

old Serbia (which was the Kosovo area, at that time). Although he was leading his people away from their homeland, he was uniting Serbs, an act that would be remembered for centuries. [20]

    In 1804, the Serbs revolted against the Ottoman Empire that had ruled for four centuries. Civil disputes occurred between two Serbian houses, the Karadjordje and the Obrenovic. The rancor culminated in the 1903 assassination of Alexander Obrenovic. Both of these Serbian dynasties had been created by men of humble background: Djordje Petrovic (aka Karadjordje or Black George), who led the first Serbian uprising in 1804, and his rival Milos Obrenovic were illiterate, dirt-poor pig farmers. Black George and Obrenovic fought against foreign powers as well as against each other. Both men created family dynasties that would rule Serbia years after their deaths. Karadjordje's political violence was legendary: he had his stepfather killed for failing to flee the Turkish invaders upon command; had his brother hung for rape — and invited Serbian leaders to his home for dinner while the body hung from the gate; and played great powers against each other while seeking their support.[21] Obrenovic, like Karadjordje, fought the Turks by gaining concessions and then undermining Turkish power.

After the Turks slaughtered and pillaged much of Serbia, Obrenovic sensed danger from Karadjordje when he returned from hiding. Karadjordje had been smuggled back into Serbia with the aid of a Greek revolutionary society, Philiki Etairia (Friendly Society). The Philiki Etairia, like Karadjordje and the Serbs, were enemies of Turkey and aimed at destabilizing the Ottoman Empire in preparation for their own armed rebellion. Obrenovic sent agents to kill Karadjordje, which they did by cutting his head off with an ax, stuffing it, and sending it to a Turkish sultan. The act exacerbated the feud between the two families.

In the mid-1800s the Omaladina (Union of Serbia Youth), a secret society of terrorists, acted to spur the downfall of the Serbian government in hopes of creating a larger Serbian nation linked with other Balkan states and parts of Poland, Moravia, Silesia, and Romania.[22] This union was to create a great, single Slavonic nation. During half a century the Omaladina committed a variety of outrageous acts including the assassination of Serbian Prince Michael in 1868, the kidnapping of Serbian Prince Alexander, and a rebellion that led to the abdication of Serbian King Milan and the murder of his successor, King Alexander Obrenovic and his wife, Queen Draga Masin, in 1903. The Omaladina's pro-Serbian ideology served as an inspiration for future Serbian secret societies like the Black Hand.

THE BULL AND KING ALEXANDER OBRENOVIC

In August 1876, Dragutin Dimitrijevic and Alexander Obrenovic were born in Belgrade at a time when Serbia and Montenegro were plotting against the Ottoman Empire and Belgrade was still paying tribute to the sultan of Constantinople. Dragutin was born in the humble home of an impoverished family; Alexander was born in a palace, the only son of King Milan Obrenovic, leader of the ancient royal Serbian family who won its position through murder and political intrigue. While Dimitrijevic would gain power through military promotion and stealthy dealings within secret societies, Obrenovic would shape Serbia by constitutional change that angered its citizenry. Dimitrijevic's record at military school was so impressive that he was immediately installed in the Serbian army as an officer. Both men would meet violently 26 years after their birth, inside King Alexander Obrenovic's palace.

    Queen Draga was ten years her husband's senior and tricked Alexander into marriage with a false pregnancy, but Alexander seemed content with a woman who was notoriously devious. She convinced Alexander that his father was plotting to remove him from the throne and have him replaced with one of his half-brothers born of his father's Greek mistress. She infuriated the army by interfering with appointments and had any officer she suspected of opposing her denied promotion. She was unable to have children and her condition placed her two brothers next in line for the throne, both of whom were also hated by the Serbs.

Apis – Dragutin Dimitrijevic

At 2 a.m. on June 11, 1903, forty military officers swarmed into the palace. Apis and Lt. Petar Zivkoc led them under the command of George Genchich, the former minister of the interior who was ousted from office after Alexander's marriage to Draga. Some accounts say that before they entered the palace the conspirators were drinking in local bars; though it is unknown whether any were drunk, it is known that Apis never touched alcohol. A palace guardsman was bribed to allow the officers access to the palace's rear entry. The royal couple hid in a closet of their bedchamber — an escape route cut into the floor of the bedchamber had been sealed in advance by Alexander. Dynamite was detonated in an effort to blast open the palace doors; at least, it blew all the fuses in the palace. With power cut, the officers searched for ninety minutes by candlelight for Alexander and Draga. Finally, they found the closet and shot the king thirty-six times and the queen fourteen, then mutilated their bodies with swords and threw them out a window. In the battle with the king's bodyguards, several men were injured or killed. Queen Draga's brothers were also slain, as was Serbia's prime minister, the minister of war, and an assistant to King Alexander. Pesar Karadjordje was installed as king — the grandson of the pig farmer, Djordje Petrovic, the original Karadjordje (Black George). The feud between the two royal houses that was ignited by Karadjordje's death one hundred years before was avenged, and the Obrenovic dynasty was over.[23]

Apis was spirited away from the palace and he recovered from his wounds. Most of the conspirators of Alexander's assassination were army officers who felt Alexander's regime had tainted Serbia's international reputation by backing a new constitution in 1901 that allowed Alexander too much power. The conspirators gave Serbia's rule to a more democratic union of political parties. The Serbian Parliament thanked Apis for his grisly deed and called him "the savior of the fatherland." His reputation won him a position as Professor of Tactics at the Military Academy. Elections were held less than four months after the assassination. In 1911, Apis began plotting a new pro-Serbian secret society in Belgrade, *Ujedinjenje ili Smrt* (Union or Death), also known to its enemies as *The Black Hand*. The organization's first goal was to incite rebellious activity against the Ottoman Empire in Macedonia.

THE BALKAN WARS

In 1866, an alliance consisting of Serbia, Montenegro, Romania and Greece made up the first Balkan League. A compromise between Austria and Hungary in 1867 recast the Austrian (Hapsburg) Empire under the name of Austria-Hungary, comprising numerous provinces ruled by a monarchy.[24] At the beginning of the twentieth century the countries of the Balkan Peninsula, the easternmost of Europe's three great southern peninsulas, were shaped and reshaped by wars between the Balkan League countries, the Austro-Hungarian Empire, and the ever-present Turks. In the spring of 1912, the Russians helped re-establish the Balkan League with Bulgaria, Serbia, Greece, and Montenegro. By 1914, Austria-Hungary and the countries of the Balkan Peninsula incorporated no fewer than eighteen different racial groups.[25]

After Obrenovic's assassination, the Serbs constituted the most dynamic element in the Balkans and the greatest threat to the Austria-Hungarian monarchy. The tensions leading up to the assassination of the Austrian archduke, and the world war that followed in August 1914, were created by two sets of wars staged in the Balkans during 1912 and 1913. On the eve of the Balkan Wars the streets of Constantinople were full of chants, "We want war," "Down with equality," and "The Balkan dogs are trampling on Islam!" The Balkan Wars eerily foreshadowed the subsequent wars of the twentieth century. They were marked by wholesale cruelty and brutality. The First Balkan War was fought between Turkey and the Balkan League with the principal goal of liberating Macedonia from the seemingly eternal grip of the Ottoman

Empire. On October 8, 1912, Montenegro declared war on Turkey and the other members followed with declarations ten days later. By attacking Macedonia and taking it away from Turkey, Russia saw an opportunity to expand its land holdings and weaken Turkey by helping the Balkan states create their own sovereignty. The Greek navy played an important part of the war when they gained control of the Aegean. Turkey agreed to an armistice in December 1912. The sweeping and decisive nature of the victory left Europe stunned; Turkey found its military forces decimated and it was left with little more than Constantinople. "Turks" was a pejorative term for Muslims during this time, and ridding Serbia of Turks was considered a necessary step in creating an ethnically homogeneous Greater Serbia.[26]

Before the 1912 conflict, Apis entered Turkish-controlled Albania and convinced top Albanian officials to support the Serbian cause for the good of a free Albania. Apis was involved in a failed plot against the life of Austria-Hungary Emperor Franz Joseph in 1911. He was also involved with a Bulgarian revolutionary group that assassinated

Ferdinand of Bulgaria in 1914 and during the subsequent world war he plotted against the King of Greece.

A second Balkan War began when the Balkan League members of Serbia, Greece, and Romania disagreed with Bulgaria on how Macedonia would be split. During the summer of 1913 a war ensued and Bulgaria was defeated, a humiliation Bulgarians would remember when they sided with Austria-Hungary and the Germans during the Great War that would follow. Bulgarians, although excellent soldiers, were hated by all their neighbors and more than once they chose the wrong side in war. The Bulgarians suffered both in the second Balkan War and World War I, because of their insistence that they were the rightful rulers of Macedonia. Macedonia's plight led author John Reed to write, in 1916, "The Macedonian question has been the cause of every great European war for the last fifty years, and until that is settled there will be no more peace either in the Balkans or out of them." Robert Kaplan followed in this vein by writing, "Macedonia is full of historical lessons, if only history were better learned or remembered."[27]

## THE OBSESSIONS OF THE YOUNG BOSNIANS

To secretly fight Austrian imperialism, the *Narodna Odbrana* (National Defense) was established on October 8, 1908, during a meeting at City Hall in Belgrade after Austria annexed Bosnia and Herzegovina into the Austro-Hungarian Empire. Among the members were numerous government officials including Prime Minister Nikola Paschitsch, the leader of the popular Radical Party. The public image of the organization was one of nationalist propaganda, but secretly the group recruited saboteurs to destroy railways and bridges. Agents were also trained in guerilla warfare. Within a month the *Narodna Odbrana* had recruited more than 5,000 volunteers prepared to cross the border into Bosnia and Herzegovina to fight Austria.

*The Black Hand* -- Charles River Editors

But the *Narodna Odbrana* eventually softened into a "peaceful cultural society restricted to modest, unobtrusive individual efforts."[28] Apis and other radicals found that the *Narodna Odbrana* was not doing what it was intended to do: to fight the Austro-Hungarian government with violent means. A new secret organization was created to fight Austria: *Crna Ruka*, the Black Hand. Ten men, including Apis, met on May 9, 1911, to help create the Black Hand. They wrote a constitution that clearly outlined the organization's purpose and designed a bizarre seal with an image of a powerful arm holding a flag, along with a skull with crossed bones, a knife, a bomb, and a phial of poison. The organization was established at the grassroots level in three to five-member cells with district committees comprising army officers, civil servants, and intellectuals. In a dark room each member was inducted over a crucifix, a dagger, and a revolver with the words, "By the Sun that warms me, by the Earth that nourishes me, by the blood of my ancestors, on my honor and on my life."[29] The organization was lent an air of credibility with Apis at its helm. He was broadly considered a man of unquestioned patriotism, charm, and selflessness.

From Belgrade the Black Hand recruited government officials and army officers as commanders. The Black Hand's purpose was similar to the Omaladina and the original intent of *Narodna Odbrana*: to create a single Serbian nation free of ruling hands from outside sovereignties. Apis steered clear of the political trappings of Omaladina. He wanted to eliminate enemies of Serbia through assassination, so he recruited young fanatics, many of whom were tuberculins with little to live for other than a brief, glorious moment — which they could, presumably, achieve as assassins for Serbia. Apis had a persuasive manner and a personal magnetism that drew other fanatics to him; two of his devotees described his as a "true man" and a "type of magician."[30]

After 1918, the assassins of Ferdinand, who belonged to numerous secret societies consisting mostly of students of peasant origin from Croatia, Dalmatia, and Serbia, were known collectively as "Mlada Bosna" or "Young Bosnians." Among the Black Hand were other secret revolutionary societies like

Sloboda (Freedom) and Matica (Mainstream). Their intent was to destroy the Hapsburg Empire and to overcome the illiteracy and primitivism of their society. Between 1912 and 1914 the Young Bosnians were involved in a dozen terrorist plots of sabotage and assassination. Though the Black Hand was involved in social reform, it was much more inclined to violence than the other societies, which placed their emphasis on intellectual pursuits, especially studies of literature, ethics, politics, and the improvement of education. The Young Bosnians were so engaged in literary activity that they convinced many people that literature was their only passion. They were known to have translated Kierkegaard, Strindberg, Ibsen, and Edgar Allan Poe. Their strange mixture of interest in literature and revolution could be compared to the French anarchists of the 1880s and 1890s, who were known for their literary ability: Emile Henry, Stuart Merrill, and Paul Valery. Czech writers Franz Kafka and Jaroslav Hasek were considered sympathizers of the libertarian literary movements in Prague.[31] Danilo Ilic, an eventual conspirator against Ferdinand with Princip, found time to translate Oscar Wilde's *Thoughts About Art and Criticism*. Ivo Andric, a Croat and Serbian sympathizer who became involved in Young Bosnian activities, was eventually arrested as a conspirator with Princip and Ilic in Ferdinand's assassination and was sentenced to three years in prison; he spent the time becoming a devotee of Dostoyevsky and Kierkegaard. In 1962, Andric won the Nobel Prize for literature, he was the only Yugoslavian to do so.[32]

In contrast to the Young Bosnians and just as fervent were the Young Turks, established in the 1860s. Their philosophy coalesced by 1902 around a fanatical desire to preserve the old Ottoman Empire as a Turkish nation-state. The Young Turks' position created friction for non-Turks including Albanians, Arabs, and Armenians. Eventually, violence by the Turks in the form of wholesale massacres of Armenians led the Balkan states to ally themselves in what would become the Balkan Wars of 1912-13; this violence would change the face of Europe drastically over the next five to six years.

In 1910, following a peasant revolt in a Croatian village, the Austrian army attacked the revolutionaries with raids throughout the region of Bosanka Krajina, Croatia. In retaliation against the Austrians, General Varesanin, the Austrian Governor of Bosnia-Herzegovina, was targeted for assassination while opening parliament in Sarajevo. Though Sarajevo was a Bosnian province ruled by Austro-Hungarian Empire, many Serbs lived there. Five shots either missed or only wounded Varesanin as he crossed the Kaiser's bridge in Sarajevo. The failed assassin, Bogdan Zerajic, then turned the gun on himself — but not before uttering the legendary (and perhaps apocryphal) words, "I leave my revenge to Serbdom." Zerajic had intended to kill Franz Joseph, initially, but had never been able to get close enough to him during his travels through Bosnia and Herzegovina in 1910. Zerajic was a member of the secret society, Sloboda, as well as a Serbian member of the Black Hand. One account suggests that Apis provided him with the pistol for the shooting and that Apis, disgusted with Zerajic's failure, had his body unceremoniously dumped in an unmarked grave.

Nevertheless, Zerajic's act was heralded by members of the Black Hand as an inspiration for the "new people, new Serbs." His body was eventually buried in a proper, marked site. Many of the members of the Black Hand vowed to avenge his death; Gavrilo Princip was a regular visitor to his grave as were his Black Hand confederates Danilo Ilic and Nedeljko Cabrinovic.[33] Four years later Princip would return to Sarajevo for his revenge. Zerajic's skull was removed from the burial spot and exhibited in the Criminal Museum in Sarajevo. The chief investigator of Ferdinand's assassination Viktor Ivasjuk allegedly used the Zerajic skull as an inkpot in his office. The chief investigator told one of the conspirators in the assassination that if he didn't admit to everything he knew about the conspiracy to kill Archduke Ferdinand, Ivasjuk would use all of the conspirators' skulls as inkpots.[34]

## THE ARCHDUKE, THE EMPEROR, AND THE COLONEL

Archduke Franz Ferdinand von Sterreich-Este was the nephew of the reigning ruler of Austria-Hungary, Emperor Franz

Joseph. As the heir to the empire, he had embodied the elegance that was typical of his aristocratic background; he was tall, corpulent, and often wore ceremonial green plumes from his helmet.[35] His marriage to Sophie Chotek von Chtokowa und Wognin angered Franz Joseph, which in turn created friction with Ferdinand. Sophie was a daughter of a Czech nobleman but nevertheless was a commoner in the eyes of the Hapsburgs, who considered her the offspring of an impoverished, simple, and common Bohemian family. Many members of Ferdinand's Vienna court viewed the marriage with Sophie as a scandal and thought that King Alexander's 1903 assassination was due to his equally scandalous marriage to the unpopular Queen Draga.

The archduke's personality was paranoid and unpleasant; he quickly became unpopular among all the classes.[36] He was well known for his bigotry and hatred for Jews, Socialists, Hungarians, Italians, and Serbs — a close friend went as far as saying that he was unbalanced in everything. His wife confided in more than one friendly ear that she feared her husband was on the verge of madness.

Rumors that he would be "removed" hinted at not only the Balkan revolutionary groups but Austria as well.[37] With a history of insanity running in his family, many Austrians wondered whether Ferdinand was mentally fit. It was also believed that he had contracted tuberculosis.

Colonel Dimitrijevic acknowledged the archduke as a dynamic leader who would eventually attack the Serbs. He suspected a pre-emptive strike aimed at ending Serbia's role as a leader in the Slavic movement. In fact, Ferdinand viewed the Serbs as an inferior race whose goal was to destroy the Hapsburg dynasty.[38]

It is author Remak's *(Sarajevo)* opinion that Apis sentenced Franz Ferdinand to death not because the Archduke was hostile to the Slavs, but because he planned reforms that might prove far too attractive to the Young Bosnians. The eighty-four-year-old Franz Joseph was deemed too old to seriously entertain the idea of invading any country, but Apis understood that Ferdinand was bold enough to undertake a military strike. By eliminating Ferdinand, Apis believed, peace could be assured, the Serbian armies could restore themselves after the devastating Balkan wars of recent years, and Russia would gladly join Serbia in an all-out war against Austria-Hungary — after all, the 1912 strike against the Turks had succeeded.[39]

A PRINCE WAITING IN AMBUSH

Gavrilo Princip's grandfather was a Slav who immigrated into the valley of Grahavo Polje in Western Bosnia from an unknown origin and occupied a house that had been vacated by Muslim Turks. Bosnian locals had recently chased the Turks out of the region. The grandfather's name was Ceka, which meant "he who waits in ambush." He wore a jacket with bells that the locals found strange but fascinating, and so they gave the man the name "Princip," meaning prince. This created an erroneous post-assassination legend that Princip's father was the illegitimate son of a prince, though he was certainly only a peasant man who married a peasant Montenegrin woman. She bore nine children, of which six died, leaving three sons: a doctor, a tradesman who became a mayor of his town, and Gavrilo.

When Princip was seventeen, he was expelled from his Sarajevo school for taking part in violent anti-Austrian demonstrations. He traveled to Belgrade and made contact with the *Narodna Obrana* in a coffee house. He volunteered for service in the Conitadjis, a fanatical group that was dedicated to fighting the Turks since long before the first Balkan War. Princip, never of robust health, made a poor impression on Major Vajislav Tankosic, leader of the Conitadjis and a compatriot of Apis (the two had played important roles in the assassination of Alexander Obrenovic in 1903). Tankosic rejected Princip from the militia group, a humiliation Princip would not forget. On March 27, 1914 Princip shook hands with another revolutionary, Cabrinovic, and they both made a solemn pledge to kill the Archduke of Austria-Hungary, Franz Ferdinand.

Gavrilo Princip first learned of the Archduke's plan to visit Sarajevo from a Croatian newspaper article that another Sarajevo Young Bosnian, Mihajlo Pusara, mailed to friend and fellow conspirator Nedeljko Cabrinovic in Belgrade in April of 1914. The envelope contained a single paragraph concerning the visit and nothing else. Borijove Jevtic said the *Srobobran* newspaper article was mailed from Zagreb, Croatia and when it "reached our meeting place, the café called Zeata Moruna [Green Garland] one night . . . [it] was the torch which set the world afire with war . . . That paper wrecked old, proud empires . . . At a small table in a very humble café, beneath a flickering gas jet we sat and read I . . . our decision was taken almost immediately. Death to the tyrant!"[40] Jevtic was a personal friend of Princip, but apparently he did not become closely involved in the assassination. After the assassination he was arrested and held in a cell next to Princip's, but told the court that Princip had never filled him in on the details and that if he had, he would have tried to dissuade him. However, Jevtic did know of the plot and said as much in his statement, after the fact: "To make his [Ferdinand's] death certain 22 members of the organization were selected to carry out the sentence. At first we thought we would choose the men by lot. But here Gavrilo Princip intervened." Jevtic was eventually dismissed on all charges.

Princip saw his opportunity and immediately began preparing for the assassination by asking a fellow student, Djuro Sarac, to help him find weapons. Sarac organized another Young Bosnian group, which he named "Death or Life," which comprised of Sarac, Princip, and five others. Princip and his group turned to Apis and the Black Hand for weapons and support. Sarac had fought in the Balkan wars under Major Tankosic, who became one Apis's most trusted aides. Initially, Apis refused to help Sarac and Princip, but finally relented and arranged for Tankosic to supply the group with Serbian Army grenades, a map of Bosnia, 150 dinars, four Browning pistols, six bombs filled with nails and pieces of lead, and cyanide of potassium for suicide. Tankosic, to avoid direct contact with the future assassins, used Milan Ciganovic, the twenty-six-year-old Bosnian, as a go-between. Princip and his Black Hand confederates prepared a single package of arms and had them sent directly from Belgrade to Sarajevo to Danilo Ilic, Princip's best friend. Princip, Nedjelko Cabrinovic, and Trifko Grabez were smuggled into Sarajevo by a chain of Orthodox families who sympathized with the Black Hand. Before Princip and his confederates left Belgrade for their fateful journey to Sarajevo, Tankosic met with them. Princip remembered how Tankosic had rejected him from service in the military and refused to meet with him. He sent Grabez to meet him instead, though what was said at the meeting is unknown.

Though warned not to travel into dangerous country, Ferdinand planned to exhibit his power on a day that was special to Serbian patriots. Numerous officials were apprehensive. Serbian Prime Minister Nikola Pasic got wind of the plot and told the Serbian Minister in Vienna, Jotza Jovanovitch, that a Black Hand assassination attempt was imminent. It is also believed that the Crown Prince of Serbia went as far as rewarding some of the plotters.[41] Anti-Ferdinand pamphlets had been circulated in Orthodox parishes in the Bosnia-Herzegovina countryside that declared, "Down with the Austrian-Este dog and the filthy Bohemian sow!"

The archduke was surely aware of the threat of violence when visiting Sarajevo. Terrorist acts were numerous at the beginning of the twentieth century. A rash of anarchist bombings and assassinations in the 1890s had made their mark: in 1894, an Italian anarchist assassinated French President Sadi Carnot; in 1897, anarchists assassinated Empress Elizabeth of Austria and Antonio Canovas, the Spanish prime minister; in 1900 the Italian King Umberto I was killed by an anarchist. Umberto's murder inspired the assassination of American President William McKinley by self-proclaimed anarchist Leon Czolgosz. (McKinley's murder in September of 1901 ushered in the presidency of the inimitable American President Theodore Roosevelt.) From 1903 to 1913, 33 major political figures were assassinated throughout the world, three in the Balkans (1907, Prime Minister of Bulgaria Nikola Petkov; 1909, Albanian politician Fehmi Effendi; 1913, King George of Greece). [42]

## JUNE 28, 1914 — IN REVERENCE FOR SERBIAN ASSASSINS OF THE PAST

The archduke visited Bosnia in order to view army maneuvers. Apis believed that the Austrian army's presence in Bosnia was the prelude to an attack on Serbia, but it is quite probable that Ferdinand had no intention of attacking Serbia. He surely realized that an attack would bring Russia into a war that would be devastating. Ferdinand may have been more inclined to establish a separate prosperous, autonomous Slavic State within the Austria-Hungarian Empire — but Apis would have feared that just as much.

The night before arriving in Sarajevo by train, the archduke and his wife slept in the resort town of Ilidza, Bosnia. The next day, June 28, 1914, they toured the Bosnian capital, Sarajevo, in the open, four-cylinder Austria-produced Graef und Stift touring car that would take them to Sarajevo city hall. The numerous Serbs living in Sarajevo were celebrating St. Vitus's Day, also known as "Vidovdan." June 28, 1914 was the 525th anniversary of the assassination of the Turkish Sultan Murad by a Serbian hero, Milosh Obilich, during the 1389 Battle of Kosovo Polje. Though the Turks won on the battlefield, the battle created a myriad of legends, myths, and Serbian heroes. The Serbs became increasingly defiant and unified against all perceived enemies.[43]

The Battle of Kosovo Polje pitted the Serbs, clad in cumbersome but ornate armor, against the lightly clad Turks mounted on swift Mongolian ponies. When defeat appeared imminent, the Serbian nobleman and soldier Milosh Obilich allegedly feigned desertion to the Turkish cause, or so one version of the story goes. When presented to the Turk commander, Sultan Murad, Obilich flung out a hidden dagger and killed the Turk. (Obilich's real name was "Kobilich," which meant "broodmare." Serbs, who thought it shameful that one of their heroes would be called "broodmare," dropped the "K.") King Peter I created a bravery medal bearing Obilich's name in 1912. Some Serbs believed that Obilich should not be honored since the assassination was accomplished through trickery but, as author Rebecca West reported, the patriots of Serbia believed that the deception was justifiable given it was intended to help destroy such a treacherous enemy.

Obilich's use of assassination in the name of Serbian independence would be celebrated and revered by many future assassins who proudly declared themselves Serbian patriots. As author Vladimir Dedijer

(*The Road to Sarajevo*) writes, Obilich for the Serbs is the "incarnation of the cult of self-sacrifice." Lavender Cassels (*The Archduke and the Assassin*) writes, "Milos Obilich became the epitome of the heroic warrior who sacrificed his life to kill the cruel oppressor; the defeat of Kosovo was portrayed as a national martyrdom, which would be followed by resurrection, and so as an inspiration for the overthrow of foreign tyrants."[44] Though Ferdinand was simply visiting Sarajevo with his wife on the battle's anniversary, which coincided with his wedding anniversary, for any Young Bosnian revolutionary the archduke was the reincarnation of the hated Sultan.

The Battle of Kosovo would later serve as a source of inspiration for Yugoslavian President Slobodan Milosevic, who made a famous appearance in front of a crowd of Serbs at Kosovo Polje on the battle's 600th anniversary in 1987. There he pointed at the legendary site of the disastrous Serbian defeat, saying, "Nobody, either now or in the future, has the right to beat you." Five months later he was elected president. Milosevic's declaration was a rallying cry for

Serbs and a prelude to the 1990s wars in Albania and Bosnia that would cost the lives of 200,000.

The imperial motorcade of six vehicles traveled along the quay of the Miljacka River, which runs through the heart of the city. Seven years earlier Franz Joseph had visited Sarajevo under extraordinary security that was not afforded his nephew. In order to protect Joseph, officials had evacuated all strangers from the town, confined all anti-Austrians in their homes, and had the streets lined with troops and detectives. For Ferdinand there were several aspiring young assassins lining the route. The seven members of "Young Bosnia" that waited in ambush were Nedjelko Cabrinovic, Vasco Cubrilovic, Trifko Grabez, Danilo Ilic, Mohammed Mehmedbasic, Cvijetko Popovic, and Gavrilo Princip. All were aged 19 to 27. Nedeljko Cabrinovic threw a grenade that bounced off the archduke's car and rolled beneath the trailing car, exploding and injuring twenty people. Cabrinovic was also armed with cyanide. He swallowed the lethal pill and ran to the river to drown himself. The cyanide was old and only made him vomit.

The river was only two feet deep due to the summer heat. He was pulled out the river only half wet and was asked who he was. "A Serbian hero," he replied.

Ferdinand and wife Sophie greeted by a Sarajevo official moments before their deaths

The archduke's car roared past the other assassins, who did nothing. Four of the conspirators abandoned their posts, leaving only Gavrilo Princip still in the area; but he too had given up hope of seeing the archduke again, so he walked across the street from his post to Moritz Schiller's café and delicatessen and ordered coffee. The car raced to the city hall where the Lord Mayor met the archduke. The archduke was outraged by the bomb but nevertheless read his speech — though the paper was soaked in the blood of his injured aide-de-camp. Then, the archduke wished to visit the hospital that was to treat the injured. Instead of having him wait for a proper escort of soldiers, the Lord Mayor suggested taking an alternate route, different from the route publicized in newspapers. The archduke's procession started for the hospital but the Lord Mayor had forgotten to tell the driver of the change in the plan, so the driver continued on the same route as advertised. The Lord Mayor told the driver to stop and back up. The car halted five feet from the Moritz Schiller café, directly in front of Princip. Princip stood up from his seat and pulled a .38 M1910 Browning pistol from his pocket, intending to shoot the archduke and the Military Governor, General Oskar Potiorek. Just as he raised his gun, a detective noticed it and began to jump between Princip and the archduke. Incredibly, a bystander saw what Princip was trying to do and kicked the detective, stopping him long enough to allow Princip to continue raising his weapon. The bystander was another Young Bosnian, Mihajlo Pusara, a Sarajevo actor and singer. How much he knew of the plot has never been entirely clear, but he was aware of

Princip's presence and his intention.[45] It was Pusara who had forwarded the newspaper article concerning Ferdinand's desire to visit Sarajevo, and his route. Princip shot twice: the deflected shot penetrated the car and Sophie's chest; the second shot hit the archduke's neck, severing a jugular vein. Both died minutes later, shortly before noon. Princip testified at his trial that he raised the pistol to his head but was unable to shoot himself; he also swallowed the cyanide but his, too, was impotent and failed to deliver him death. Onlookers pummeled him until he was arrested.[46]

What was Princip's state of mind as he stalked the archduke? In the year 2000, *Smithsonian* writer David DeVoss interviewed Lubica Tuta, eleven years old at the time of the assassination. She said, "I knew his girlfriend, Jelena Milisic. Jelena and Borislav Mihacevic were Young Bosnia revolutionaries with Gavrilo. Boro used to tease Jelena about spending the night with Gavrilo in the park across the river from where the attack occurred. Gavrilo desperately wanted to make love, but Jelena said no. Even when he told her he probably would die the following morning, she wouldn't relent . . . Gavrilo was so angry the morning of June 28 that he would have shot God himself."[47]

Whether Apis ever physically met Princip is unclear but Apis's desire to bring Princip and his radical brethren into the Black Hand as cheap and discardable tools was obvious. Apis biographer MacKenzie writes that Princip, Cabrinovic, and Grabez were too young to be allowed to join the Black Hand, which did not allow "minors."

It did not matter whether Apis ever met the Ferdinand assassins; his will was clearly guiding them. Princip may have only been part of the minor group "Death or Life," but he and his confederates acted with the same calling as the Black Hand: to free the Slavs from the oppressive rule of the Hapsburgs. The Black Hand and the Young Bosnians sought to eliminate Ferdinand but for reasons that were different, if ever so slightly. The Young Bosnians detested the Dual Monarchy of Ferdinand's Austria and Hungary and wished to live in the idyllic world of a Pan Slavic nation, a Yugoslavian federation. Apis and his Black Hand feared that Ferdinand would try to create a "Greater

Serbia" by attacking Serbia and establishing Hapsburg rule over an ersatz federation of Slavs.

INVESTIGATING THE ASSASSINATION

Ferdinand and Sophie's death caused little concern to his uncle, the ruling monarch of Austria-Hungary. The elderly Franz Joseph must have thought it was just one more strange circumstance in his life, like the assassination of his wife and the murder or murder-suicide of his son. He commented optimistically that his nephew's death would probably act as a pacifier in the ethnically troubled domain. Germany's Kaiser Wilhelm II responded to the assassination in an equally equable manner. Most Americans probably shared the opinion of a Grand Forks, North Dakota editorialist with the *Daily Herald* who mistakenly wrote, "To the world, or to a nation, an archduke more or less makes little difference."[48] Political assassination and unrest in the Balkans had become so commonplace that the archduke's death was not mentioned in the London *Times* until July 21st. From the beginning of the new century a political assassination had occurred in the world on an average of once every four months.

Initially, Princip and Cabrinovic kept quiet about the attack. Danilo Ilic was captured in a roundup of subversives. He volunteered some information. On July 5, three other conspirators were arrested. The investigation was mismanaged, governed by a petty police judge in Sarajevo. They found weapons supplied by Milan Ciganovic and knew that Colonel Apis, the chief of Military Intelligence of the Serbian General Staff, had helped in passing along information and arms to the conspirators. On June 29, riots broke out in Sarajevo with Croats and Moslems attacking the Serbs. By July 5, all the conspirators had been rounded up and arrested. The Catholic Hapsburgs took their revenge on Orthodox Serb peasants, rounding up hundreds and slaughtering them.

## THE TRIAL OF PRINCIP AND THE BLACK HAND CONSPIRATORS

Princip and his Black Hand companions had initially planned on murdering high Austrian officials, especially in Bosnia; their hatred focused on General Oska

Potiorek, the Military Governor of Bosnia. Apis convinced them that "one must strike the snake in the head," by killing Ferdinand, not the replaceable governors or generals. Removing Ferdinand, Apis argued, would doom the monarchy's regeneration and reorganization and would remove the main obstacle to Serbian unity.

During the trial, after the short introductory passage of a pamphlet concerning the failed and martyred assassin Zerajic was read, Princip, when asked by the judge what he had to say about the text, shouted, "Hail to Zerajic! Hail, and nothing else!" The trial ended October 23, 1914. Of the twenty-five accused, three were hanged on February 3, 1915: Danilo Ilic, Veljko Cubrilovic, and Misko Jovanovic. Nine were set free and the rest were sentenced to long prison sentences. Princip was sentenced to twenty years at hard labor with the proviso that he spent each June 28 of his term without food or water in a darkened cell. He was spared execution due to his age: he was supposedly under the age of twenty on June 28 but no one was really sure of his birth date.[49] Jovanovic had helped smuggle the weapons into Bosnia. Veljko Cubrilovic was a teacher who had helped smuggle the assassins into Bosnia. Ilic was one of the seven along the quay and had visited the hero Zerajic's grave along with Princip during the days when Ilic was translating Oscar Wilde.

Princip (middle front row) and Young Bosnian co-conspirators at trial

Six of the seven Young Bosnians who lined the quay, waiting for the archduke, were arrested and convicted. Princip told the police, "I recognized the heir apparent. But as I saw that a lady was sitting next to him, I reflected for a moment whether I should shoot or not. At the same moment I was filled with a peculiar feeling and I aimed at the heir apparent from the pavement — which was made easier because the car was proceeding slower at the moment. Where I aimed I do not know . . ." Mehmed Mehmedbasic, a Bosnian Muslim, alone escaped prosecution.[50]

Princip told the court that, if one were trying to find that "someone else had instigated the assassination, one strays from the truth. The idea arose in our own minds, and we ourselves executed it." Princip died of tuberculosis in the hospital of Theresienstadt prison in April 28, 1918; the walls on his cell are marked with his poetry: "Our ghosts will walk through Vienna / And roam through the palace / Frightening the lords." His body was secretly buried but later was found and moved to a grave built beneath a chapel at St. Mark's Cemetery in Sarajevo with the remains of other conspirators; the site was marked as a burial place for the "heroes of Vidovdan [the murder of Sultan Murad, St. Vitus's Day]." With the recent breakup of Yugoslavia, the burial site has been ignored and is unkempt. For years, a modest black tablet was set on the wall of a building overlooking the site of the assassination, "so high above the street level that the casual passer-by would not remark it." It read, "Here in this historical place, Gavrilo Princip was the initiator of liberty, on the day of the St. Vitus, the 28th of June, 1914." Princip, whose life has been the topic of a novel, remained a cult hero for years until

Serbs attacked the people of Sarajevo in the 1990s.[51]

THE AUSTRIAN ULTIMATUM AND RUSSIAN TREACHERY

On July 13 a secret report made by Austrian agents was dispatched to Vienna, claiming that the Serbian government had had no role in the assassination. At the same time a German ambassador to London wrote a letter to a Berlin colleague, blaming the Austrian authorities for sending Ferdinand to an "alley of bomb throwers" even though the Serbian Foreign Minister had warned Austria that a visit would be unwise.[52] On paper it appeared there was little sentiment or reason for Austria to rationalize a war against Serbia. However, July 23, 1914 Austria issued an ultimatum to Serbia. Serbia was given until July 25th to accept the terms. Serbia was to immediately publish a declaration condemning terrorism, suppress and dissolve terrorist organizations, and arrest Serbian Milan Ciganovic, Major Vajislav Tankosic, and Colonel Dragutin Dimitrijevic. [53]

The ultimatum was designed to be rejected, so that it would provide a reason for Austria to invade and subdue Serbia before wider repercussions developed. The Austrians were right about the rejection and disastrously wrong about the repercussions. The Serbian government did reject the ultimatum. In fact, many of its intelligence agents, including the head of military intelligence, Apis, had indeed been involved with the Black Hand and were instrumental in the planning and execution of the assassination. The Austrians mobilized their forces along the border, poised to strike at Serbia. On July 28, Austria declared war. Historian Martin Gilbert professes, "few documents have had such an impact on the twentieth century as the Austrian ultimatum to Serbia." Only the Treaty of Versailles, wrote Gilbert, and Hitler's autobiography

*Mein Kampf* compare in their impact on history.[54]

The assassination of Ferdinand left the Russians in a predicament. Although technically an ally of Serbia, Russia was not unlike Austria-Hungary in its ambitions to subjugate and control the small country. Russia could remain passive, but then it would be perceived as an impotent European power that would remain ineffective, as was the case in the Balkan Wars; or it could stand with Serbia and risk a challenge from the alliance of Germany, resulting in a major conflict. The Russians moved troops along the German border. Kaiser Wilhelm II protested the mobilization to his cousin Nicholas II, czar of Russia. The Czar's war minister (Sukhomlinov) and chief of the general staff (Yanushkievich) told the czar that they not only had mobilized their forces along the German border but were planning to do the same along Austria's borders. Nicholas ordered the troops be withdrawn from the German border immediately but Sukhomlinov and Yanushkievich kept the troops in place, while indicating to the czar that they had been moved. The czar telegraphed Wilhelm to say that the troops had been removed; when Wilhelm found out otherwise, he naturally assumed his cousin was lying to him. Wilhelm declared war on Russia.

On August 1, 1914, the mayhem officially began. Germany declared war on Russia, and then on France on August 3. On August 4, Germany invaded Belgium and Britain declared war on Germany. For continental Europe, Germany and Austro-Hungary could mobilize seven-and-a-half million armed soldiers and the Russians and French ten million. France was a member of the "Triple Entente," the three European super powers under alliance — Great Britain, Russia, France. France sought revenge for her 1870-1871 defeat at the hands of Germany; Russia likewise saw a way to reconcile her humiliation at the hands of the Japanese by siding with the Slavic people and expanding their boundaries at the expense of the Slavs' enemy, the Turks. Britain sought a balanced Europe so it could continue to exploit her vast colonial empire. Alliances doomed Europe to war: Russia joined Serbia, Germany sided with Austria-Hungary, France with Russia, Great Britain with France, and eventually the US with Great Britain and France.

If there were any doubt about the US's neutrality concerning the war, it was dashed when the British allegedly intercepted a telegram from Berlin to Mexico in January of 1917. With both sides deadlocked, the Germans were seeking new allies: Japan and Mexico. The "Zimmermann" telegram urged Mexico and Japan to attack the US. Berlin promised Mexico that it would recover lost land in the form of Texas, Arizona, and New Mexico. What Japan would gain was not entirely clear. The sinking of the *Lusitania* gave Wilson the official impetus for entering the war as an act that would "make the world safer for democracy." The US Congress voted to go to war with Germany on April 7, 1917, four days after Wilson addressed the Congress with a speech in which he said, "We enter this war only where we are clearly forced into it because there are no other means of defending our rights." On December 7, 1917, the US declared war on Austria-Hungary. The Americans' fervor was fanned by the great propaganda machine in Hollywood. Films like *The Kaiser: The Beast of Berlin*, *Pershing's*

*Crusaders,* and *To Hell With The Kaiser* were wildly popular in 1917 and created angry mobs outside theaters when the overflow crowds were denied admission. While Hollywood refined the motion picture as an art form and propaganda tool, a German soldier, Erich Maria Remarque, was experiencing the real war and would later write the novel, *All Quiet on the Western Front*, which would become renowned as an anti-war book and eventually an award-winning movie.[55]

## THE DEMISE OF THE BULL

Apis avoided apprehension and prosecution for Ferdinand's murder, but he was not forgotten. Serbian Regent Prince Alexander and Prime Minister Pasic, both of whom believed Apis was plotting to assassinate them, feared him. They also accused him of negotiating secretly with the Germans for a separate peace treaty, but little evidence has been found to substantiate the charge.[56] By 1916, it seemed credible that Germany and Austria would win the war and take over Serbia. Pasic feared that the Serbian government's role in the plot to kill Ferdinand would be discovered; he conceived a scheme to kill Apis, under the direction of a General Zivkovitch and another secret society, aptly called White Hand. Zivkovitch hired a henchman to poison Apis but the hireling lost his nerve.[57]

Apis was arrested on December 15, 1916 with other leading members of the Black Hand and was charged with planning to assassinate Alexander and Pasic, secretly drafting a peace agreement with Germany, and inciting a mutiny in the army in order to switch to the German cause. His chief aide, Major Vajislav Tankosic, had recently been killed in military action defending Serbia. Apis was tried for treason in 1917 in Thessaloniki, Greece. Concerning Ferdinand's death he testified that the Serbian "government was kept informed of the doings of the organization [Black Hand], that the foreign minister knew and approved." Though he was accused of plotting to kill Alexander and Pasic, there was no evidence. Their investigators tortured several members of the Black Hand, including Mehmed Mehmedbasic, and all stubbornly refused to say that Apis had plotted against the prince or prime minister. Only Rade Malobabic (who had smuggled grenades into Sarajevo for the Ferdinand attack but escaped before being prosecuted) broke under torture and accused Apis of plotting against the prince and prime minister. Malobabic, arrested in the Ferdinand plot, was kept in chains until November, 1915. When the Serbian Army was forced to abandon the territory where Malobabic was being held, he was freed. Apis took pity on Malobabic, who had suffered considerably in prison, and kept him as an aide until their arrest.

Apis was found guilty of treason and executed by firing squad on June 26, 1917, along with Rade Malobabic and Jamor Ljudomir Vulovic. The Bull shouted, "Long live Serbia! Long live Yugoslavia!" before he fell. Ferdinand's and Dimitrijevic's life were contrasted in a 1932 novel, *Apis und Este*.[58]

UNPRECEDENTED WORLD CARNAGE

The First World War created the greatest carnage in world history up to that time and laid the foundation for the Second World War. With the war came colossal battles whose names will live for decades (if not centuries) to come: Verdun, Ypres, Gallipoli, Somme.[59] Sixty-five million soldiers, sailors, and airmen were involved. Disease killed one-sixth of the soldiers.[60] There were 8 million military deaths, 6 million civilian deaths, 21 million wounded at a cost in early twentieth-century dollars of almost $282 billion.[61] Another account puts the military dead at 10 million, with a cost of $337 billion.[62]

In August 1915, the Turks used the chaos of the war as a cover for attacking the Armenians. Though Turks and Armenians had lived as peaceful neighbors for centuries, the Turks dreamed of a Pan-Turkish empire while the Armenians longed for the ideal Christian-based autonomous state. The Turks "solved" the Armenian problem by killing as many of them as possible, mostly by "relocating" the Armenians in what amounted to a death march. More than 1.4 million Armenians were killed. When the Allies learned of the slaughter in 1915, they announced that the Turks would be held responsible for "crimes against humanity," the first use of the term. Author Peter Balakian has said that no history of World War I can be understood without understanding what the Turks did to the Armenians.[63] Ex-President and Nobel Peace Prize winner Theodore Roosevelt called the Armenian genocide "the greatest crime of the war." Various Armenian militants struck back at the Turks throughout the following decades. One group, the Armenian Genocide, was created in 1975 and claimed responsibility for the murder of Turkish diplomats.

"When the twentieth century began," wrote historian Martin Gilbert, "assassination was regarded as one of the evils of the nineteenth century that would not be perpetuated in 'modern times.' The handiwork of a discredited ideology — anarchism — assassination was thought to have no place in the new century."[64] Though survivors of the "Great War" looked back in nostalgia at the felicitous time of a "Long Peace" during the beginning of the twentieth century, when the war started British citizens in their sixties had already seen 24 wars throughout the world, though they were brief and peripheral to the British citizenry.[65]

PRINCIP, OBILICH, AND ZERAJIC —
ASSASSINS PASSING THE TORCH

What were Princip's real motives? Some historians have considered that it was the perfect political murder, and suggest it is impossible to know the true motives and truth; but Princip may have thought of himself as an avenging Serbian hero like the legendary Milosh Obilich, the Serbian assassin-hero of the Battle of Kosovo, and Bodgan Zerajic, the failed assassin whose grave was a regular visiting place for Princip before his act in Sarajevo. Like the hero-assassin Milosh Obilich, Princip has been memorialized with a name that was not originally his, and like Obilich he used a hidden weapon to assassinate an enemy of Serbia. Neither doubted his resolve nor reason in acting out his murders. A variety of countries and secret societies have been blamed for complicity in the archduke's murder including the Bolsheviks, whom Alfred von Wegerer, a Sarajevo assassination expert, identified as instigators. He based the theory on the words of Bolshevik leader Karl Redek, who said in 1937 that Princip was an example of a political prisoner who kept his secret to the end. Though Leon Trotsky, the compatriot of the Bolshevik leader Vladimir

Ilyich Lenin, claimed he was opposed to individual terrorism, he had visited Serbia in 1914 and had been acquainted with members of the Black Hand. Czarist Russia has also been named as a possible conspirator with reports that the Czar's secret police, *Ochrana*,[66] infiltrated the Young Bosnians and encouraged violent acts against Austria and possibly aided Apis in the plot.[67] A transcript of the trial reveals a possible connection between the Black Hand and the much-maligned society of Freemasons.[68] In 1914, the British Foreign Secretary recognized that "the world will presumably never be told all that was behind the murders . . ."[69] On May 12, 1916, a doctor asked Princip if he believed the assassination was a service. Dr. Pappenheim's notes read, "Cannot believe that world war was a consequence of the assassination; cannot feel himself responsible for the catastrophe; therefore cannot say if it was a service. But fears he did it in vain."

    The Communist regime headed by Josip Broz (Tito) boosted Gavrilo Princip's reputation as a hero. A Princip museum was opened in 1953 at the corner where he made his historical stand against Ferdinand and the

Austrians. The Young Bosnian Museum was a shrine to Princip's memory as well as other conspirators of his age. A bridge was named after him and impressions of his footprints were placed in the spot where he fired the shots. When the Serbs attacked Sarajevo in 1992, the citizens turned on the Young Bosnian Museum, stealing and smashing artifacts. The museum represented the former Yugoslavia. The surviving material of the museum was moved to another location but some items like the clothes Princip wore are still available for viewing. In April of 2003, the museum was refurbished with a city donation of $33,000 so that the shooting could be documented in the "context of Bosnia under Austrian rule at the turn of the century."[70] Ferdinand's and his wife's bodies were laid to rest in the "Franz Ferdinand Museum" in lower Austria within Artstetlen Castle.

Otto von Bismarck, the heroic Chancellor of the Second Reich of Germany, feared assassination himself and carried a revolver. Bismarck was chairman of the June, 1878 Congress of Berlin, a month-long meeting of European powers that helped create alliances, for better or worse. With a recent Russian victory over the Turks, the Treaty of San Stefano awarded Macedonia to Bulgaria. Bismarck found this unacceptable, fearing too much Russian influence within the region. The Congress of Berlin delegated Macedonia back to Turkish rule. The borders of Montenegro and Serbia were considered irrelevant to the welfare of Europe. The agreement in Berlin allowed the Turks to stay in Macedonia, raping and torturing girls, it was said, "with boiling oil and hot irons. They stole cattle, broke into stores, and buried people in mud inside pigsties for not paying exorbitant taxes."[71] Macedonia, wrote Balkan Wars scholar Andre Gerolymatos, was a microcosm of the Balkans, a mosaic of Muslims, Christians and Jews, Greeks, Bulgarians, Serbs, Albanians, Vlachs, and Gypsies, with all the past of war and genocidal atrocities so characteristic of the region.[72] After essentially ignoring the Balkans, Bismarck remarked that war would erupt some day because of "some damn silly thing in the Balkans."

The Great War did not end until November 11, 1918 with the Versailles Treaty, an agreement that helped set up bitterness in Germany and the necessary factors to start the second "Great War." The Great War had become truly the first world war when non-European countries like Japan, China, and the US joined along with the colonial alliances of Britain: Indian, Kenya, Canada, and Australia. In 1919 French General Ferdinand Foch said of the Versailles Treaty that he helped draft, "This is not a peace treaty, it is an armistice for twenty years."[73] Twenty years later the Second World War began. "The First World War," wrote John Keegan, "inaugurated the manufacture of mass death that the second brought to a pitiless consummation."[74]

## THE IMRO, THE IRA, AND DADA

Historians Burg and Purcell wrote about the reason for starting the Great War: "In essence, the war had come about because a handful of politicians thought they could improve the lot of their nations by means of a short, decisive conflict."[75] As authors Audoin-Rouzeau and Becker put it, the Great War became "a paradigm case for thinking about what is the very essence of history: the weight of the dead on the living."[76] The central paradox of the war, they wrote, was that it was waged by each side in the belief that it would "bring a new and radiant world in the future" and rid humanity of its most horrible flaw, war: thus it was the war to end all wars. The tremendous loss of life was unbearable and created a rise of spiritualism, especially in England. Celebrated writer Sir Arthur Conan Doyle lost his son, his brother, a brother-in-law from his first marriage and three brothers-in-law from his second marriage. Rudyard Kipling lost his son and devoted much of his time to a memorial dedicated to his son. Both writers tried to communicate with the dead through séances; Doyle devoted much of his time to the pursuit of understanding various aspects of the occult.[77]

Social changes caused by the war were profound: the war ended the ancient Hapsburg, Romanov, Hohenzollern, and Ottoman dynasties — empires that had ruled Europe for centuries. While the war raged in 1917, Russia's political scheme was drastically altered by the Bolshevik Revolution. In November of 1917, the Balfour Declaration committed Britain to help establish a Jewish homeland in Palestine, an act that has had profound impact on the world ever since. One of the first champions of a Jewish state was journalist Theodor Herzl, who tried to garner international support at the First Zionist congress in August, 1897. It seems ironic that Herzl came from Austria, considering the Hapsburgs of Austria's impact on World War I and the influence another Austrian, Adolf Hitler, would have on the Second World War and the future of the Jewish people in Europe and Palestine.

Another secret organization created in 1893 in Thessaloniki, Greece (also known as Salonika, named after Alexander the Great's half-sister), the Internal Macedonian Revolutionary Organization (IMRO), was devoted to "creating political, economic, and social chaos," which would make the country unsafe for European investment and force the Ottoman Empire to grant the region autonomy.[78] Thessaloniki was the launching site for Alexander the Great's famous conquests and, centuries later, Apis's trial. The IMRO's first enemy was the Ottoman Empire. Like that of the Black Hand, the chaos created by the IMRO failed to lead to an autonomous Macedonia. After the second

Balkan War the IMRO switched its purpose to recovering lost lands of Macedonia. While secret societies like the Black Hand faded into obscurity, the IMRO flourished into the twentieth century with killers swearing allegiance over a gun and an Orthodox Bible and attacking, among others, Serbs, in some cases murdering entire staffs of schools in the 1920s and 1930s. A strong contingent of the IMRO worked in Bulgaria after World War I, dedicated to recapturing from the Yugoslavs and Greeks what they perceived as their part of Macedonia. In the 1930s an assassination could be ordered through the IMRO for $20. The most famous chieftain of the IMRO was Ivanco Mihailov. He agreed to marry his wife only if she killed his rival, which she did.[79]

While trench warfare raged on the European continent, Irish Catholic organizations started a rebellion during the Easter week of 1916. Taking advantage of Britain's preoccupation with the war in France, armed Irish men occupied government buildings in Dublin. British troops eventually quelled the riot but not before killing 1300 people, an outrage that galvanized radicals into the Irish Volunteers and eventually the Irish Republican Army (IRA) in 1919.

A significant figure in the Easter week uprising and the subsequent fight for independence was Michael Collins, an Irishman born in West Cork. He was second in command under Joseph Plunkett during the Easter Week uprising. In 1917, Collins became part of Sinn Fein, the so-called first political party of Ireland. Within the Sinn Fein network Collins helped create an intelligence network, a national loan to fund a rebellion, an assassination squad ("The Twelve Apostles"), and an arms-smuggling operation. The first recruits were warned that their "work would not be suitable for anyone who had scruples about taking a life." The Twelve Apostles, also known as The Squad, targeted British agents and their sympathizers.[80] The Squad was officially founded September 19, 1919. Like Dimitrijevic, Collins was an intelligence officer who created an assassination squad and had a fanatical devotion to the cause of nationalism. Both men died violently — Dimitrijevic by state execution and Collins by assassination, an act still shrouded in mystery. The Nazis made an effort to ally themselves with the IRA in 1940 by recruiting members for sabotage against the British.[81] The IRA, and the IMRO that was established in the late nineteenth century, are among the oldest terror organizations in Europe, distinctive in their longevity and use of violence coupled with the use of legitimate political mechanisms.[82]

The need to express the horror and futility of the war gave rise to a unique body of expression in the form of Dadaism. George Grosz, a German artist, became swept up in the call for duty and enlisted in the German Army in 1914. Quickly he learned what all other soldiers learned. Instead of being bathed in the shining light of heroic deeds and easy victories, Grosz was engulfed in what he called the filth, idiocy, and deformity of the war. Grosz was medically discharged, recalled to service, seemingly went mad, was accused of being a deserter, and eventually was admitted to a mental hospital. He began drawing his hatred and disillusionment of the war: men cursing the moon, soldiers without noses, war cripples with crustacean-like steel arms, a skeleton dressed as a recruit. Grosz' anti-war sentiment soon made him a target of the German government. In major European cities like Zurich and Paris, Grosz, Hugo Ball, Richard Huelsenbeck, Tristan Tzara, Marcel Duchamp, Andre Breton and many others began working in the "Dada" movement, staging "demonstrations" that consisted of readings and drawing exhibitions as well as producing Dada magazines (*Every Man His Own Football, The Bordello, Rose-Colored Glasses*). Dadaism, once claimed by Tzara as the "ism of isms," was first a reflection of the horrors war imposed on the human psyche, then it became anti-war, then anti-manifesto, then an inspiration for new abstract painters (Klee and Kandinsky), a voice for anarchism and pure nonsense, an inspiration for the surrealism art movement, and finally an "ism" declared dead and meaningless by its own inventors.[83]

## A KARADJORDE ASSASSINATED — VLADA THE CHAUFFEUR

On October 9, 1934 the Serbian born King of Yugoslavia, Alexander Karadjordje, was assassinated in Marseille as he drove in an open touring car similar to the one Ferdinand had used in Sarajevo. This time the conspiracy was traced to a Bulgarian hit man, Vlada

Cherozamsky,[84] who was in league with the pro-Catholic Croatian nationalist terrorist group, Ustasha, headed by Ante Pavelic.[85] Like Princip's killing of Ferdinand, the Ustasha and the IMRO thought the assassination of Alexander would end Serbian rule over their beloved Croatia and Macedonia. The Ustasha would take an influential role in the genocide of Orthodox Serbs as it joined in a murderous coalition with the Nazis of the 1940s.

    From a hospital bed in England, British novelist and journalist Rebecca West listened to a radio news flash describing the death of Alexander. Wondering if Alexander's death would trigger another European conflict, as soon as she was back on her feet she set out to investigate the Balkans. A six-week journey through the area in 1937 resulted in a remarkable work, *Black Lamb, Grey Falcon — A Journey Through Yugoslavia*. This half-million word book published in 1941 examined the Balkans more deeply than anyone had done to date. West, born Cicily Fairfield in 1892, was a prolific and forceful writer during her ninety-year life, which was punctuated with a ten-year relationship with writer H.G. Wells and her acclaimed study of the Balkans. No serious study of the Balkans can omit Rebecca West's work, which was immediately heralded as a literary masterpiece and described as a polemical pro-Serbian travel diary. West describes numerous aspects of the clash between the archduke and the Black Hand within her lengthy tome, and includes her meeting with Cabrinovic's sister. The sister denied that Cabrinovic had tuberculosis at the time of the assassination, though he did die of the disease in prison. Some writers had written that Cabrinovic's father was an Austrian spy though there seems, according to West, little to substantiate the claim.

*Black Lamb and Grey Falcon – A Journey Through Yugoslavia*, Rebecca West

Inspired by West's book, Robert D. Kaplan published *Balkan Ghosts — A Journey Through History* in 1990, just months before Yugoslavia broke out into another set of bloody conflicts. *Balkan Ghosts* is a combination of historical analysis, political reporting, and travel book. In 1993, President Clinton read the book when he was contemplating taking action in the Balkans. Kaplan's description of the ethnic rivalry reportedly "encouraged the President's pessimism about the region," wrote Kaplan in the foreword of a later edition of the book, and was a "factor in his decision not to launch an overt military response in support of the Bosnian Moslems," besieged by the Bosnian Serbs.

Winston Churchill wrote for the *News of the World* on May 30, 1937 concerning the assassination of Ferdinand that "The 28th of June, 1914, was to the great majority of those whose lives it changed, a day like any other. Yet, for years past, the current of European affairs had been flowing towards the abyss."

# Chapter 2. The Assassination of JFK

Lee H. Oswald

"After he fired the last or the third shot, he didn't seem to be in a great rush, hurry. He seemed to pause for a moment to see if for sure he had accomplished his purpose, and he brought the gun back to an upright position as though he was satisfied." – Howard Brennan assassination witness

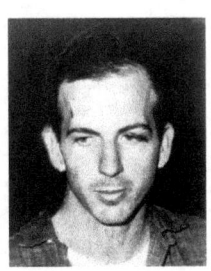

Oswald

On November 22, 1963 at 12:30 p.m., US President John Kennedy's midnight-blue Lincoln convertible limousine entered a grassy park area called Dealey Plaza on its way through the streets of Dallas, Texas to the city's Trade Mart for a luncheon. The Kennedy administration had hoped that a motorcade would evoke a demonstration of the president's popularity in a city that he lost in the 1960 presidential election. As Kennedy, Texas Governor John Connally, and their wives waved to well-wishers, rifle shots cracked through the air. Both the president and the governor were hit. The president was fatally injured; the governor survived his wounds. Kennedy was the fourth American president to be assassinated. If Oswald really killed Kennedy, and if he was acting on his own, the four assassins of American presidents were inspired by four quite different political leanings: one was a Democrat, one a Republican, one an anarchist, and one, as best we can tell, a Communist.[86]

The source and number of shots fired has been argued for decades. The official investigating body of the assassination, The Warren Commission employed a full-time staff of 28 people for ten months and produced a ten-million-word, 26-volume study based on 26,550 interviews, but even so, they failed or were unable to interview a number of important witnesses. They concluded that there were three shots fired at the motorcade. The Commission stated that whether the shot that hit Kennedy in the neck was the first or the second could not be determined.[87] They also concluded that all those shots were fired from an Italian Carcano model 91/38, 6.5 mm. rifle[88] operated by twenty-four-year-old Lee Harvey Oswald of Dallas. From the first moment, the public has feared a conspiracy in the assassination. Gov. Connally screamed, "They're trying to kill us all," as the limousine picked up speed on its way to Parkland Hospital. Conspiracy theories have run the gamut, implicating the Soviets, Cuban intelligence, the CIA, FBI, Cuban exiles, French hitmen, the Mafia, LBJ, J. Edgar Hoover, Texas oilmen, the Dallas Police

Department, various US military intelligence agencies, and the Freemasons.[89] The Zapruder film, an 8-millimeter home movie shot by a parade by-stander named Abraham Zapruder, clearly documented the final head shot to the president; it may be the most closely scrutinized piece of film in history.

In a 1976 article concerning assassination reporters, author Nora Ephron wrote that smart reporters of the day stayed away from this story because it ". . . begs for hundreds of investigators, subpoena power, forensics experts, grants of immunity; it's also a story that requires slogging through 27 volumes of the Warren Commission report and dozens of books on the assassination." Since Ms. Ephron wrote this in 1976, there has been the 1978 U.S. Congressional investigation (House Select Commission on Assassinations) that added another 12 volumes as a companion piece to the Warren Commission's study. Subsequently, countless news articles, books, essays, Web sites, magazines, academic journals, Web blogs, film documentaries, Hollywood movies, speculative novels, and scrutiny of every centimeter of film frame or still photograph taken in Dealey Plaza that day have added to the case's complicated nature.[90]

A 1975 congressional investigation produced several acoustic studies of a Dallas police dicta-belt recording executed within Dealey Plaza at the time of the shooting.[91] Provable evidence that a multiple-gun conspiracy was accomplished in Dealey Plaza was dashed when it was realized that *no recording* within Dealey Plaza during the shooting ever existed. The Warren Commission and supporters of the Commission's findings have described the accused assassin, Lee H. Oswald, as a loner and a Marxist who had inadequate social skills and a miserable marriage. However, he had numerous ties with organizations and individuals linked with the activities to pro-Communists and anti-communists, Cuban exiles, American right-wing groups, and the Mafia. One of the most intriguing of these relationships was with the brilliant misfit David William Ferrie of New Orleans.

LINCOLN, FERDINAND, AND KENNEDY

The assassination of President Abraham Lincoln by John Wilkes Booth is also riddled with mystery. Booth was a famous Shakespearean actor who had planned to kidnap Lincoln at one time and eventually shot the president with a pistol in Ford's Theater in Washington D.C. only days after General Robert E. Lee's famous surrender at Appomattox. Conspirators alleged to have aided Booth were executed. Booth wrote in his diary the day before the murder, "I can never repent it, though we hated to kill: Our country owed all her trouble to him and God simply made me the instrument of his punishment." Booth, like fellow murderer Jesse James, has been loosely linked to The Knights of the Golden Circle (KGC), a mysterious secret society that Warren Getler called the "most powerful subversive organization ever to operate within the US." The KGC has been accused of planning the first salvos against Fort Sumter in April of 1861 that started the American Civil War and of plotting to overthrow both the Mexican government and the post-Civil War federal government. Booth allegedly took the vows of the KGC in a room of a castle in Baltimore where portraits of Jefferson Davis (once president of the Confederate South) and

Stephen Douglas (one-time leader of the Illinois Democratic Party) hung. Like the Black Hand and other secret societies, the KGC used a mysterious ceremony to shore up the resolve of its members. In Booth's case, he was fighting "Yankee domination" and vowed to "risk all to help Southern Independence."[92]

There are certain similarities between the assassinations of Archduke Franz Ferdinand of Austria in 1914 and US President John F. Kennedy in 1963. Both men were traveling in a southern region where they were unpopular; both were accompanied by their wives when they were shot; both were in open, state-of-the-art automobiles and accompanied by the local governor (also similar to King Alexander of Yugoslavia's death in 1934); their deaths were quick and were orchestrated by several people and possibly several organizations working in concert; in some cases the existence of so many conflicting stories, the impenetrable inconsistencies in witnesses' testimony and peculiarities in the government follow-up seem to suggest that government figures were involved.

Ferdinand's death has throughout the years been clearly linked to a radical organization, the Serbian Black Hand. Though Ferdinand's death has been at the very least indirectly linked to the detonation of the First World War, Kennedy's death did not set off such a great cataclysm — though one was feared. Still, it is possible the Vietnam War may not have been escalated if the president had lived to serve out his term of office. Howard Jones (*Death of a Generation — How the Assassinations of Diem and JFK Prolonged the Vietnam War*) wrote, "the only person in the Kennedy administration who consistently opposed the commitment of US combat forces was the president."[93] However, in the days immediately after the assassination there were real fears that this might be the first shot in another world war, a horror that was expressed to President Johnson by Secretary of State Dean Rusk. US military forces were brought to an alert status of DEFCON3 on the afternoon of the assassination.[94] The assassination shocked the world and led German journalist Ulrike Meinhof, who would later become part of a radical terror group in Germany, to write: "The grief fades, the emptiness remains. The man the nations of the world believed would make peace is dead . . . we must not go backwards but find other, alternative ways . . ."

Just as the investigating bodies of the Serbian government studied the relationships of assassin Gavrilo Princip, the life and relations of Lee Oswald, Kennedy's alleged assassin, have been fodder for endless research and speculation.[95] Though Princip's motive for killing Ferdinand was clearly stated, Oswald's motive has never been clear. Princip's actions were part of a conspiracy of the secret society, the Black Hand, guided by a Serbian government official, Dragutin Dimitrijevic with the possibility of help from other sources like the Bolsheviks and Czarist Russia. Did Oswald have a similar relationship with a mentor who guided him to action, or was he an agent of the Fair Play for Cuba Committee, an organization that allegedly consisted of only one person — Oswald?

OSWALD'S CURIOUS ACQUAINTANCES

Who did Oswald know? He had few friends. A domineering mother raised him after his father died two months before his birth in 1939. He spent ages three through five at the Evangelical Lutheran Bethlehem Orphan Asylum (also called the Bethlehem Children's Home) because his mother was unable to care for him. A 1993 interview of one of the boys who was at the institution at the same time as Oswald showed a two-year stay that had a detrimental effect on Oswald. Allen Campbell described the institution as a "house of horrors" where children were fed water and four-day-old bread, and the boys, including four-year-old Oswald, watched from a crawl space above the room as a priest sexually assaulted the older girls. The girls, afraid of being killed, asked the boys to watch. "I know it affected all of us tremendously," said Campbell. "We would go into a state of depression for days and days after."[96] Oswald's family circumstances appear offer some parallels to those examples of infamy with whom he was eventually equated: Sirhan Sirhan, James Earl Ray, Arthur Bremmer, Charles Manson, and Theodore Kaczynski all grew up fatherless.

During his childhood and teens he, his stepfather Edwin Ekdahl, mother, and brother moved many times. He joined the

Marines and made such an impression on one of his fellow Marines, Kerry Thornley, that Thornley wrote a novel (*The Idle Warriors*), months before the assassination — with Oswald as the basis for the main character.[97] After his stint in the Marines and his defection to Russia, Oswald returned to the United States disenchanted with both Russia and his birthplace the US.

Novel *The Idle Warriors* by Thornley

Marina Prusakov was encouraged by her uncle Ilya to attend a trade union dance at the Palace of Culture in Minsk in mid-March 1961. It was there that the pretty nineteen-year-old met Oswald. A mere six weeks later they were married. Whether this whirlwind romance was true love or some kind of arrangement has been a source of wonder to many writers. Marina's uncle was Colonel Ilya

Prusakov, a member of the Soviet internal security agency, MVD, the same Soviet agency that supposedly provided living expenses for defectors like Oswald. A CIA document declassified in 1976 and dated December 1963 stated that a CIA agent was informed by a Soviet consul general at a Soviet embassy that Oswald was "sent to USSR and married Soviet girl under CIA instructions."[98] This set of queer circumstances has led to the speculation that the CIA was interested in getting Ilya Prusakov to defect, though he never did. Lucienne Goldberg, who later became a literary agent and exposed US President Bill Clinton's problems by befriending and tape recording Monica Lewinsky, is the only person to have interviewed Lee Harvey Oswald in the Soviet Union.[99]

George deMohrenschildt was an unlikely character to link up with Oswald. DeMohrenschildt, a suave and sophisticated businessman with acquaintances in the CIA and a variety of intelligence services, was Russian born. His father was of German descent, though George obscured the fact by changing his name from "Von" to "De." It was the Russian background that supposedly brought the deMohrenschildts together with the Oswalds. DeMohrenschildt told interviewer Jay Edward Epstein that he was asked to learn as much as he could about Oswald and his stay in Russia for his friend J. Walter Moore, a member of the CIA's Domestic Contacts Division. DeMohrenschildt said, "Lee Harvey Oswald was smart as hell. They make a moron out of him . . . ahead of his time . . . a kind of a hippie . . . too good in his knowledge of the Russian language not to have been instructed by someone. And I will tell you this — I am sure he did *not* shoot the president."[100] On the other hand, when deMohrenschildt learned that the president had been shot on November 22, 1963, the first thing he asked was if the suspect's name were Lee Oswald, claiming that his question was based on a subconscious hunch because he knew Oswald had a gun.[101] DeMohrenschildt allegedly had ties with German, French, and Polish intelligence services as well as friendships with right-wing oilmen. In 1941 he had established a relationship with a distant cousin, Baron Konstantin von Maydell, in hopes of creating documentary films. Maydell at the time was the senior resident agent of the Nazi military intelligence service, *Abwehr*, and spent the rest of the war years interned in North Dakota under a cloud of suspicion. DeMohrenschildt had intelligence and oil relationships with George H.W. Bush in the early 1960s; Bush's address and his company Zapata Petroleum are cited in one of DeMohrenschildt's notebooks.[102] In the mid-seventies, deMohrenschildt began to suffer extreme bronchitis and paranoia. In 1976, he wrote an unpublished manuscript on Oswald entitled *Patsy! I Am a Patsy!*, based on remarks Oswald made to newsmen on the evening of November 22, 1963 at a Dallas police station. The night he completed it he tried, unsuccessfully, to commit suicide by swallowing tranquilizers. In 1977, following an interview with Epstein, deMohrenschildt shot himself. Also in 1977 he admitted that a CIA agent in Dallas had asked him to "keep an eye on the Oswalds" when they had returned from Russia.[103] Epstein believed deMohrenschildt was despondent over the possibility of being forced to testify to the House Select Committee on Assassinations

(HSCA), an opinion shared by HSCA investigator Gaeton Fonzi, the man who left his card at the house where deMohrenschildt was staying only hours before deMohrenschildt killed himself.[104]

George deMohrenschildt

Along with deMohrenschildt, Oswald has been linked to the Korean War hero, military intelligence officer (1955-59), CIA contract agent (1962-63), and alleged double agent Richard Nagell who had himself arrested in an El Paso, Texas bank robbery on September 20, 1963.[105] Nagell told police officer Jim Bundren, "I'm glad you caught me. I really don't want to be in Dallas." He didn't elaborate at the time but later revealed he had met Oswald in Mexico City and in Texas, and sent a registered letter in September of 1963 to J. Edgar Hoover (which was never acknowledged), claiming that there was a plot to kill President Kennedy that involved Oswald,[106] and that while assigned to penetrate Soviet intelligence by the CIA, he was ordered by the Soviets to assassinate Oswald before he could murder Kennedy. Though the Warren Commission never mentions Nagell, he was the main topic of a two-hour interview with Marina Oswald by the Secret Service.[107] There are numerous connections between Oswald and Nagell,[108] none being more significant than Nagell's claim that he was asked by the CIA to investigate Oswald and an anti-Castro organization called Alpha 66.[109] Nagell told Dick Russell that he was assigned by Soviet intelligence to monitor an assassination plot to kill JFK. The source of the plot was never revealed but the Soviets wanted him to monitor Oswald, as well. The Soviets had nothing to gain by the death of JFK, and they had much to lose if an ex-citizen of the U.S.S.R. were to be linked with such a plot. This fear, Nagell believed, was the reason that the KGB had ordered him to kill Oswald. This led Nagell to remove himself from the web, and get himself into custody before he could be implicated further, himself.[110] Nagell's claims are still considered unreliable by many researchers. Nagell went through harrowing events in his life: wounded three times in battle, two military plane crashes where he was the only survivor, and espionage work in various theaters both domestic and foreign. He and Oswald shared many experiences: both were from broken homes, had done military service, were interested in Marxism, apparently worked with American and Soviet intelligence, and are revealed through psychiatric analyses to have potentially unstable minds; and both were linked to the assassination of the president.

Other acquaintances were Jerry Patrick Hemming, a mercenary soldier involved in anti-Castro activities; he was questioned by the FBI concerning a Johnson 30.06 rifle that is said to have been found in Dealey Plaza after the JFK assassination. Hemming claimed he met Oswald in Los Angeles, where Oswald told him he was a radar operator who was "helping the Cubans out with everything he knew."[111] David Atlee Phillips, aka Maurice Bishop, a CIA agent involved in anti-Castro activities, was seen speaking with Oswald just weeks before the assassination, though Phillips denied meeting Oswald.[112] Investigator Penn Jones received a letter from Mexico City in 1975 from an unknown source. The letter was handwritten and endorsed to a certain "Mr. Hunt," dated November 8, 1963 and linked to Oswald, who supposedly wrote, "I would like information concerding [sic] my position. I am asking only for information . . . we discuss the matter fully before steps are taken . . ." A note accompanying the letter written in Spanish said a copy was sent to the FBI as well.[113]

Then there is David Ferrie, Oswald's Civil Air Patrol instructor, who claimed he never knew Oswald. Ferrie has been linked to the CIA and to New Orleans businessman Clay Shaw (the only man put on trial for complicity in the assassination of the president); he worked for the known anti-Kennedy Mafia kingpin Carlos Marcello, and allegedly was engaged in group conversations in which he vehemently advocated the assassination of John F. Kennedy.

David Ferrie

FERRIE AND THE NEFARIOUS

David Ferrie's life before and after the assassination is full of mystery and puzzling behavior. Cuban exiles christened him the "master of intrigue." Jim Garrison, New Orleans D.A. during the Sixties, called him a key figure in the assassination of the president and "one of history's most important individuals." Garrison's theory that Ferrie was part of a four-man assassination team that included Clay Shaw and Oswald was mentioned in a March 2, 1967 White House phone conversation between Governor John Connally and President Johnson.[114] Robert Morrow, a CIA contract employee from 1959 to 1964, claims he worked with Ferrie on many CIA covert operations and believes that Ferrie was the "mastermind" behind the assassination.[115]

Raymond Broshears, who claimed he was a roommate of Ferrie's, declared that Ferrie confided details to him concerning Ferrie's role in the assassination. A former Ferrie associate, Jack Martin, contended that Ferrie was part of a plot to kill the president — only to withdraw his assertions and say that he was only imagining things. The Secret Service showed an almost immediate interest in Ferrie following the assassination. Ferrie's activities and enigmatic behavior became a subject of concern for the 1978 House Select Committee's investigation of the assassination, citing "several parallels in the lives of the two [Oswald and Ferrie]...: complex personality and political beliefs; difficulty in achieving normal social adjustment; and a pattern of visiting the same locality at the same time, and engaging in similar activities."[116]

At the time of the assassination, Ferrie was a forty-five-year-old New Orleans resident. He possessed assorted talents and eccentricities. He was a pilot, having learned to fly in Cleveland at Sky Tech Inc. from 1942-45. He was a senior pilot with Eastern Airlines, until he was fired for homosexual activity on the job. He was also a hypnotist, accomplished pianist, a researcher of the origins of cancer, amateur psychologist, and a victim of a rare disease, alopecia, which made him lose his body hair. He listed his name in the telephone directory as Dr. Ferrie by right of a doctorate degree in psychology from an unaccredited school, Phoenix University of Bari, Italy. He was anti-Castro, anti-Kennedy, and anti-Communist; Ferrie was also a bishop of the Orthodox Old Catholic Church of North America. His odd lifestyle was embellished by an equally odd appearance, featuring a red toupee and false eyebrows. Investigator and Harrison Livingstone met Ferrie and remembered him as "an intense and sinister, cynical, disgusting, disheveled individual who was excited at the prospect of preying upon the vulnerable, the helpless, and the innocent."

Ferrie had not always been anti-Castro. In the fifties he flew guns to Castro's rebel forces as they fought Bastista's army in the Sierra Maestra. In August 1959, Miami custom agents who believed he was involved in gun smuggling put him under surveillance.[117] After a twenty-six-hour surveillance and background investigation, Custom agents notified FAA officials that Ferrie was "not involved in any nefarious acts of wrongdoing." In 1961, he flew bombing missions over Cuba and sometimes made daring landings to retrieve anti-Castro resistance fighters. When Castro announced his intentions to become a Communist, and aligned his political philosophy with Khrushchev's Soviet Union, Ferrie turned against him.

The development of Communism in Cuba, and Kennedy's inability to do anything about it, drove Ferrie to become a vociferous opponent of the president. He turned against Kennedy during the Bay of Pigs debacle, though in 1960 he had voted for Kennedy and was proud that a Catholic could win the presidency. His July 1961 speech before the New Orleans chapter of the Military Order of World Wars was cut off when he became too critical of Kennedy.[118] Ferrie became a member of the anti-Castro Cuban Revolutionary Front, an organization financed by New Orleans Mafia boss Carlos "The Little Man" Marcello and organized by Sergio Arcacha Smith. By late April 1961 the Cuban

Revolutionary Front became the Cuban Revolutionary Council (CRC). An FBI report from that month indicated that Marcello had contributed funds to Smith's anti-Castro organization in exchange for promises of concessions in Cuba after Castro's overthrow. The House Select Committee on Assassinations (HSCA) stated that, based on the evidence available to it, anti-Castro Cuban groups were not involved in the assassination but that did not "preclude the possibility that individual members may have been involved."[119] The HSCA investigated the most violent and frustrated anti-Castro groups and their leaders, selecting from more than 100 Cuban exile organizations in existence in November 1963.[120]

SERGIO ARCACHA SMITH, GUY BANISTER, AND THE CREATION OF LEGENDS

Ferrie worked extensively with Sergio Arcacha Smith in counter-revolutionary activities. Ferrie had even built two miniature submarines, which he planned to use in an attack on Havana Harbor.[121] He was questioned by the FBI on August 22, 1961 concerning the submarines and stated that he was "working with, and assisting, the Cuban Revolutionary Front, which is under the leadership of Sergio Arcacha Smith, 207 Balter Building, New Orleans, Louisiana, off and on since November 1960."[122] In an interview with Gus Russo, Smith declared Ferrie a wonderful man, "who truly wanted to help our cause. He was a gentleman. He loved to play with my children. He was a good Catholic who only wanted to help. He wanted to fly into Havana harbor and bomb the refineries. Ferrie had an idea to make two-man made submarines [built from the tanks of B-47 wings], to go in, and just blow [the refineries] up. We actually made two of them, but we were prevented from using them."[123]

The HSCA discovered[124] that in the summer of 1963, Ferrie became involved with Smith, Gordon Novel, and Layton Martens and others associated with New Orleans private investigator Guy Banister in a raid on a munitions dump in Houma, Louisiana, owned by the Schlumberger Company. The men took the stolen munitions to Banister's office at 544 Camp Street. Novel claimed that the raid was not an illegal act but had been arranged by the CIA as part of *Operation*

*Mongoose*, an official operation against Cuba developed by the National Security Council with the blessing of JFK in November of 1961. Novel lied to the FBI about the CIA's involvement in the Houma theft, because Novel felt he was expected to lie about it. In a suit against *Playboy,* for having published Jim Garrison's claim that Novel was with the CIA, Novel testified that Guy Banister and Sergio Arcacha Smith worked under CIA operative David Atlee Phillips. Novel in the same testimony admitted that he had known Clay Shaw since 1959.

Ferrie befriended Layton Martens through the Civil Air Patrol. Ferrie recruited him to work for the CRC as a fundraiser. Martens carried a letter from Robert Kennedy that stated, "These persons are acting legitimately on behalf of the US government. Please extend to them any courtesy that you can in good faith." Eventually, the letter was stolen from him; he believed Ferrie had taken it, thinking that Martens was too young to carry such an important document. Martens clearly believed that Ferrie was working for Robert Kennedy as a fundraiser "for the refugee assimilation here in New Orleans."[125]

Martens, in a 1998 interview with Gus Russo, shed some light on Ferrie's relationship with New Orleans prosecutor Jim Garrison. "For years, Ferrie had been trying to put Garrison in jail. Dave had helped Guy Banister compile 'the bomb' on Garrison. Garrison never forgave him for it." The "bomb" was a thick file of allegedly incriminating evidence against Garrison that Ferrie kept in a briefcase. According to Martens, on November 25, 1963, Ray Comstock of Garrison's office entered Ferrie's apartment without a search warrant and removed the "bomb" file.[126]

HSCA investigator Gaeton Fonzi investigated a possible link between CIA operative David Atlee Phillips and Oswald. It is Fonzi's belief that Phillips and another CIA man, Maurice Bishop, are the same person. An ex-accountant, Antonio Veciana, worked as a Cuban freedom fighter with the anti-Castro Cuban exile group Alpha 66 and was involved with CIA operations through Maurice Bishop. Veciana told Fonzi that he had seen Bishop talking to Oswald in the lobby of a Dallas office building in late August or early September of 1963. Though Oswald was residing in Louisiana at that time,

Fonzi believes there are specific periods of time when Oswald's whereabouts are unknown, specifically September 6–9, 1963.

In March, 1962, Ferrie began work as a private investigator for G. Wray Gill, Marcello's New Orleans attorney. This arrangement continued through 1963. Ferrie worked extensively for Marcello and Guy Banister, an anti-Communist ex-FBI agent whose office at 544 Camp Street (also known as 531 Lafayette) in New Orleans was also the home to a variety of right-wing and anti-Castro organizations. It has been suggested by Weberman and Canfield that CIA agent E. Howard Hunt helped Sergio Arcacha Smith link up with Banister.[127] Mark Lane also linked Hunt to a plot to assassinate JFK and Hunt sued him for it. Hunt won, but the decision was reversed in a 1985 trial. Banister had a colorful professional past that included involvement in the capture and killing of John Dillinger and work with Naval Intelligence. He conducted background investigations of CRC members for Smith. Gerry Patrick Hemming, a gun for hire, identified Banister as the man who, in September 1962, offered him a contract to assassinate JFK.[128] Banister died of a heart attack in the summer of 1964. The HSCA reviewed his files and found Oswald's name linked to the Fair Play for Cuba Committee. Guy's brother Ross, a Louisiana State policeman, said that Guy "had mentioned seeing Oswald hand out Fair Play for Cuba literature on one occasion." Ross Banister theorized that Oswald had stamped the 544 Camp St. on his literature to embarrass his brother.[129]

Ferrie worked with Banister at the same time he was employed with Gill. Ferrie, Banister, and Oswald all frequented the Mancuso Restaurant on the first floor of 544 Camp St, and may have met there.[130] Part-time private investigator Daniel L. Lewis told Garrison that he was drinking coffee with Banister's secretary Delphine Roberts when a Cuban exile, Carlos Quiroga, who was involved in the Cuban Revolutionary Front, walked in with a man he introduced as Leon Oswald. A few days later Lewis said he entered Banister's office and stumbled onto a meeting between Banister, Ferrie, Quiroga, *Leon* Oswald and another person.[131] Though the owner of the building at 544 Camp St., Sam Newman, told the HSCA that he had not rented office space to Oswald,[132] former Banister undercover worker Dan Campbell told Jim DiEugenio in a 1994 interview that Oswald was assigned an office in the summer of 1963 at 544 Camp St.[133] Guy Banister's secretary Delphine Roberts told Anthony Summers that at least once Oswald and Ferrie went together to a Cuban exile training camp near New Orleans for rifle practice, though her credibility has rightly been questioned.[134]

In February of 1967, a New Orleans policeman claimed he had stopped Oswald and Ferrie in a car together near the military training grounds of Lake Pontchartrain early one morning in the fall of 1963 (it would have to have been early fall, because Oswald spent most of that season in Dallas). One of the men identified himself as Oswald, but the police officer was not clear on how the other man identified himself. Since then he has identified the other man as Ferrie. Though the officer took the men to headquarters, they were released due to insufficient evidence of any wrongdoing.[135]

Cuban intelligence chief General Fabian Escalante told Claudia Furiati that, "in New Orleans, in April and May 1963,

Oswald's primary activity in the Banister unit was as Ferrie's assistant in the traffic of weapons for Pontchartrain. Banister also realized that Oswald was the perfect person to set up a pro-Castro front."[136] If Banister had any kind of "business" relations with Oswald or Ferrie, the purpose of a relation begs some questions: Why would an anti-Castro ex-FBI agent work directly with (1) Oswald, a Soviet defector who had supported pro-Castro activities, and (2) Ferrie, a rabidly anti-Castro self-styled investigator with links to a major Mafia figure (Marcello)? Were Oswald's activities designed to create a specific intelligence persona, or "legend"? Peter Dale Scott has developed a theory concerning the manipulation of not only Oswald, but Ferrie as well. Scott contends that Martin's false accusations against Ferrie were orchestrated by Banister to set up a legend that would help camouflage what was going on. "Ferrie was most probably in the same position as Oswald: an employee of a private investigation, who at some point was hired, probably unwittingly, to create a record or 'legend' falsely linking himself to the assassination."[137]

CIVIL AIR PATROL

Though Ferrie officially denied knowing Oswald, it is widely believed that he met him far before their alleged liaison at Camp Street. Both Ferrie and Oswald were members of the Louisiana Civil Air Patrol in 1955. Ferrie was asked to leave the air patrol just before Oswald joined, but apparently he remained close to the members of the organization. A former schoolmate claimed that he, Oswald, and Ferrie all worked in the Civil Air Patrol. Edward Voebel told the Secret Service, "when he joined the CAP, Capt. Dave Ferrie, a former pilot or co-pilot for Delta or Eastern Airlines, was the commander." [138]

Several other members of the Civil Air Patrol also said that Oswald and Ferrie were in the organization at the same time. A photo taken by John Ciravolo in the summer of 1955 at a Civil Air Patrol picnic shows Ferrie and Oswald together.[139] Roy McCoy, a former member of the same CAP, called the FBI on November 27, 1963 and told agents about a phone call his wife received from Ferrie on that day. Ferrie was "seeking information about Oswald and photographs of Oswald to show that he was not acquainted with Oswald."[140] Another CAP member, Jerry Paradis, told the HSCA, "Oswald and Ferrie were in the unit together. I know they were because I was there. I specifically remember Oswald. I can remember him clearly, and Ferrie was heading the unit then. I'm not saying that they *may* have been there together, it is a *certainty*."[141]

## JACK MARTIN'S ACCUSATIONS

Ferrie's name was first tied to the Kennedy assassination during an FBI interview between agent Jerry P. Stein and New Orleans private investigator Jack S. Martin, on November 25, 1963. Martin told the FBI that Ferrie had a relationship with the accused assassin Oswald. This certainly must have been unwelcome news to the FBI. The day before, the only suspect in the case had been murdered — and now there were others to investigate. Martin's claims seemed in equal parts disturbing and outrageous. He claimed that Ferrie had instructed Oswald in the use of a rifle; he may have hypnotized Oswald and ordered him to shoot the president; he had seen rifles like the one Oswald supposedly killed the president with in Ferrie's apartment; and Ferrie was in Texas on the day of the shooting, acting as Oswald's getaway pilot — an allegation that proved to be false. [142]

In 1978, Martin told the HSCA that on the afternoon of November 22, 1963 he was having drinks with Guy Banister when their discussion began to revolve around long distance phone calls and politics. The two returned to Banister's infamous 544 Camp St. office, where they came to blows after Martin's off-hand remark, "What are you going to do, kill me like you all did Kennedy?" Banister became furious and beat Martin with a pistol. Martin called the New Orleans police but later declined to press charges.

At approximately 3:30 p.m. on November 22, only two hours after the assassination, Ferrie rushed to Oswald's former landlady, Mrs. Jessie Garner, in New Orleans and asked if she knew anything about a library card with his name on it that Oswald might have used. Ferrie then rushed to an ex-neighbor of Oswald's and again asked if she knew anything about the card, but again he got no answer.[143] If Ferrie never had any contact with Oswald, why would he be so concerned; and unless the media quickly published or broadcast Oswald's exact New Orleans address, how would he have known where Oswald had lived? Ferrie seems to have been afraid the authorities would find out about their friendship and he may have wanted to destroy something else among Oswald's effects that would show they knew each other. As John Canal says, Ferrie probably made up the "innocent sounding" library card story because he couldn't ask Garner to allow him to search Oswald's room "for anything that had to do with exiles or CIA-Mafia assassination plots."[144] However, the library card story would come back to haunt Ferrie. Canal proposes that the story was passed on to the New Orleans police. Immediately following the "search" for the bogus library card, Ferrie made a phone call to Houston to reserve a room at the Alamotel, a motel owned by Carlos Marcello. The library card story quickly made its way to the FBI and Marcello attorney C. Wray Gill, who visited Ferrie's apartment at 1 p.m. on November 24, 1963 and told Ferrie's friend Layton Martens that Oswald's wallet contained a library card with Ferrie's name on it.

Guy Banister's office, 544 Camp St., New Orleans, Louisiana

When asked why he took the trip to Houston, Ferrie told federal authorities that he and two male companions drove all night on November 22, 1963, 350 miles, through a fierce thunderstorm to Houston to go goose hunting in Texas. The purpose of the trip was "rest and relaxation."[145] He also claimed the trip was designed to gather information on how to run an ice skating rink, a business he wished to open in New Orleans. On November 23, Ferrie visited the Winterland Skating Rink managed by Chuck Rolland. But Rolland told authorities he never spoke to Ferrie about the skating rink business. All Ferrie did, said Rolland, was make and receive phone calls for hours, at a pay phone. Records from the motels Ferrie used during this trip show two calls to radio stations WSHO and

WDSH in New Orleans and a collect call to the Town and Country Motel, Marcello's New Orleans headquarters.[146] Was this visit to Houston the first leg of a trip to Dallas designed to eliminate Oswald, on Marcello's orders, or was he supposed to act as a getaway pilot, was it an innocent recreational trip, or something else?[147]

A teletype from the New Orleans FBI office to FBI headquarters informed Director Hoover that Carlos Marcello's attorney G. Wray Gill had notified Ferrie about the library card. An inventory of Oswald's personal property by the Dallas P.D. shows no record of a library card. On the evening of November 23, 1963, Ferrie drove to Galveston, stayed the night, and returned to New Orleans the next day. Noel Twyman suggests that there may be a possible connection between Ferrie and Oswald's assassin Jack Ruby, through Ferrie's trip to Galveston after the ice-skating rink episode. He writes that Ferrie was in Galveston the same time that Ruby called (11:44 p.m. November 23) his friend Breck Wall at Thomas McKenna's house. Twyman does not elaborate on why Wall and McKenna would be involved, but he sets forth a theory that Ferrie could have passed the word from Marcello through Wall that Ruby was to eliminate Oswald.[148]

Why was Martin accusing Ferrie?[149] As previously mentioned, Banister might have been trying to create a suspicious persona for Ferrie, but it should also be noted that Ferrie had physically thrown Martin out of Gill's office in May of 1963, so that Martin may have harbored a grudge against Ferrie. A Secret Service report concluded that "information furnished by Jack S. Martin to the effect that David William Ferrie associated with Lee Harvey Oswald at New Orleans and trained Oswald in the use of a rifle" was "without foundation." The report further stated that Martin had the appearance of an alcoholic, and had a reputation of furnishing incorrect information to law enforcement officers. Additionally, Martin told the FBI that his information about Ferrie and Oswald was "a figment of his imagination and that he had made up the story after reading the newspapers and watching television."[150]

THE MANY FACES OF WILLIE O'KEEFE

Oliver Stone's film *JFK* created a fictional character, Willie O'Keefe, to tell the many stories of four real people: Perry Russo, Raymond Broshears, Dave Logan, and William Morris. Logan and Morris provided stories linking Shaw and Ferrie together, but under closer investigation their stories have been found fictional.[151]

Raymond Broshears, who claimed he was an ex-roommate of Ferrie, said that Ferrie had told him that he went to Houston the day after the assassination to await a call from a man who was, allegedly, one of the gunmen. This man was to fly from Dallas to Houston in a twin-engine plane that would take them to Central America and eventually to South Africa, where the US government had no extradition treaty. Ferrie was to serve as a co-pilot for the gunmen and another companion who was purportedly deeply involved in the assassination. The men had code names; the only one Broshears could remember was "Garcia." Ferrie said he never received the phone call. Ferrie told Broshears that the assassins panicked and tried to fly non-stop to Mexico, but they crashed off the coast of Corpus Christi and perished.[152]

Broshears told Dick Russell in 1975 that Ferrie believed Kennedy was a Communist. Ferrie had told him that he knew Oswald and that he felt Oswald did not shoot the president. Ferrie thought that Oswald believed he was working for Castro, but in reality he was a pawn in an anti-Castro conspiracy. The plotters wanted to make the assassination look like it was a communist conspiracy.

In 1963, Ferrie told Broshears that four people would shoot from different angles. Later in 1964 he said one fired from a sewer opening, another from the grassy knoll, and one from behind the motorcade. Funding for the plot came from Marcello, Ferrie told Broshears, and Clay Shaw knew many things about the plot but did not engineer it. Broshears may have never been a roommate of Ferrie; none of Ferrie's friends remembers Broshears; and his truthfulness has been questioned in every detail. Garrison realized that the information Logan, Morris, and Broshears provided concerning Ferrie could not be substantiated and he refused to have them testify at the trial. However, it was a different story with Russo.

In September 1963, Perry Raymond Russo, a New Orleans insurance agent, attended a party at Ferrie's apartment. In an interview with a Garrison aide, Assistant DA of Baton Rouge Andrew Sciambra, in February 1967, Russo detailed how, after the party broke up, a group of anti-Castro Cubans began talking of the possibilities of assassinating Fidel Castro. Ferrie introduced Russo to a tall, distinguished-looking white-haired man named Clem Bertrand; Garrison believed that was an alias of Clay Shaw. Whether Russo really encountered Shaw became the subject of an acute controversy during Garrison's of Clay Shaw. Ferrie also introduced Russo to a bearded man named Leon, whom Ferrie said was a real nut about guns. The conversation eventually drifted to the subject of Kennedy's inability to control the communists in Cuba. Ferrie dramatically took the floor and discussed the possibility of killing Castro; he illustrated his points by showing a map of Cuba, where the assassination team could land, and the routes to and from Havana. Sciambra quoted Russo as saying, "Ferrie became obsessed with the idea that an assassination could be carried out in the U.S. . . . He was the kind of person who could successfully plan an assassination . . . He was the key to the availability of [an] exit as he could jump into any plane under the sun and fly it out of the country to a place that would not extradite, such as Cuba or Brazil." Russo also recognized a picture of Sergio Arcacha Smith when Sciambra presented it to him; Russo's brother Steve recognized Smith as being associated with Ferrie.

Russo spoke of Ferrie's weird weekly black masses where he wore a black toga, worshipped with a chalice of animal blood, induced friends into hypnotic trances, and called himself a priest of the "American Eastern Catholic Orthodox Church." Russo additionally claimed that Ferrie tried to hypnotize him. Russo said Ferrie at one time spoke of killing Kennedy and blaming it on Castro, to give anti-Castro activists an excuse to invade Cuba. An assassination followed by an invasion would achieve two of Ferrie's goals — the demise of Castro and Kennedy — and open Cuba to free enterprise. He believed Kennedy could be killed by a triangulation of rifle fire. Ferrie elaborated, saying that two shooters would create diversionary shots and the third shooter would make the kill.[153]

In interviews with authors Patricia Lambert and Gerald Posner during the 1990s, Russo confessed that he thought Shaw was completely innocent of any complicity in the assassination, that Garrison should have never prosecuted Shaw, and that if he were on the Shaw jury he would have voted for Shaw's acquittal.

## CLAY SHAW

Shaw categorically denied ever knowing or meeting Oswald or Ferrie during his testimony at this trial in New Orleans. He did admit to knowing Ferrie's roommate, Layton Martens, but denied knowing that Martens was acquainted with Ferrie. Nicholas and Matilda Tadin testified to the contrary at his trial. The Tadins knew Ferrie as a flight instructor for their teenage son. In the summer of 1964, they saw Ferrie and Shaw exit from a hangar at Lakefront Airport in New Orleans. Nicholas Tadin quoted Ferrie as saying that Shaw was a friend of his and that he was in charge of the International

Trade Mart. Shaw's attorney questioned the Tadins' testimony, but it was never proven false. Another report that Shaw and Ferrie may have known each other came from a HSCA report claiming that Ferrie had flown a "high official" of Freeport Sulphur Co. (possibly Robert Kennedy's friend, former Senator Paul Douglas) to Cuba along with Clay Shaw.[154]

It is well known that Oswald used the alias of A.J. Hidell. Clay Shaw, the subject of Jim Garrison's New Orleans investigation into the assassination, used an alias of Lambert. House Select Committee on Assassinations records released in 1993 revealed a flight plan (HSCA RG 233) dated April 8, 1963, that names the pilot as "Ferrie," flying three passengers: Hidell, Lambert, and Diaz, from New Orleans to Garland, Texas. This would appear to be a very important document linking Ferrie, and the known alias of Oswald (Hidell), and the alleged alias of Shaw (Lambert), though it was never mentioned in the Shaw trial. On November 8, 1978 the HSCA asked Garrison whether the document came from his files, and Garrison said on that he believed it did. The only other comment he had about the flight plan was that it "looked quite credible" but that he and his investigators were unable to determine if it was genuine.

Though Shaw and Ferrie denied knowing each other, two photos taken in 1949 show both men together at two different social gatherings.[155] The HSCA disclosed that Shaw and Ferrie flew to Montreal in the fall of 1963. The HSCA speculated that Ferrie and Shaw were there to meet Major Louis Mortimer Bloomfield, who was a board member of Centro Mondiale Commerciale (CMC). Bloomfield was allegedly a close confidant of J. Edgar Hoover and the principal recruiter for the FBI's Division Five counterintelligence section, and a confidant of the Canadian William Stephenson, "the Man Called Intrepid," and the man thought to be responsible for recruiting Mafia hitmen to eliminate German spies during World War II. CMC was an international trade organization centered in Rome; it was a CIA front organization used for international secret spying and a classified information communications conduit among countries where the CIA operated.[156]

Vernon Bundy, a self-confessed heroin addict, testified at the Shaw trial that he saw Shaw meet Oswald along Lake Pontchartrain one day in June 1963 — while Bundy was shooting heroin. In testimony only two weeks after Shaw's arrest Bundy described "Oswald" as a "real junkie," and said his name was "Pete."[157] Bundy's testimony provided some interesting observations: that Shaw gave Oswald money; Oswald said, "What am I gonna tell her?"; a Fair Play for Cuba leaflet fell from Oswald's pants as he stuffed the money into his pocket; Shaw had a twisted walk (due to a bad back, Shaw did walk with a halting gait); Shaw arrived at the lake in a black limousine, which sounded similar to the limousine witnessed in Clinton during the voter registration incident.

An affidavit accompanying the HSCA RG 233 document claims that Georgian Edward J. Girnus stated in 1967 that one of Clay Shaw's aliases was Lambert. Girnus told Assistant District Attorney James Alcock that he had met with Clay Shaw and Oswald in New Orleans during April 1963 to discuss the purchase of guns. Shaw told Girnus that he knew people who wanted to buy guns.[158] After

Shaw made a phone call, Oswald and unknown man entered the office to discuss the deal. Girnus also said he saw Shaw and Oswald at a party held at an old colonial house he thought was owned by Shaw.

Alvin Beauboeuf, one of Ferrie's friends who accompanied him on the mysterious Houston ice rink trip, claimed Garrison investigators offered him $3000 and a job with an airline if he agreed to further link Shaw with Ferrie. Fred Lemanns, owner of a New Orleans Turkish bath, alleged that Garrison had offered to finance a private club for him if he would sign a statement maintaining he had known Clay Shaw as Clay Bertrand and that Shaw and Oswald visited his establishment.[159] The HSCA discovered that the CIA had planted a number of agents on Garrison's staff. According to Victor Marchetti, CIA director Richard Helms was concerned about Garrison's investigation and thought that he might open some doors that the CIA would prefer to keep closed.[160]

Layton Martens told Gus Russo, "Between Morris Brownlee, Al Beauboeuf, and Alan Campbell, one or more of us were at Dave's apartment practically every night that year [1963]. None of us ever heard any talk of killing Kennedy, none of us ever saw Clay Shaw, and none of us remember a Perry Russo . . . I know that Garrison actually paid Russo $5,000. He offered $10,000 to Al Beauboeuf." Garrison said to Martens, at a meeting at Garrison's house, "Here's what I want you to say: you saw Ferrie and Oswald. If you play along, you can have money, a good job, cars . . ." Beauboeuf's attorney secretly taped one of Garrison's staff offering him a bribe.[161]

GENERAL WALKER, NIXON, AND COLONEL RIVERA

On April 1, 1963, Oswald was fired from his position from Jaggars-Chiles-Stovall as a photo developer. While he had been working there, Oswald used the equipment to develop photos Marina had taken of him in their backyard as he held the socialist newspaper *The Militant* and his infamous Mannlicher-Carcano rifle. One of these photos appeared on the cover of *Life* magazine after the assassination. On April 10, he told Marina he had been fired. He wrote a note, listing eleven items to help Marina if he was "alive and taken prisoner." Marina read the note and became concerned when Lee was still away from the house until a little before midnight. When he did get home, Marina testified to the Warren Commission, he told her he had taken a shot at General Edwin Walker, and then buried the rifle.[162]

Oswald's Model 91/38, 6.5 Carcano that was fitted with the Mannlicher *en bloc* ammunition clip (not shown) and 4X Hollywood telescopic scope

Walker was a Korean War hero who had been forced to retire due to his radical rightwing comments concerning the government. Indeed, at 9:10 p.m. that night, someone had fired a rifle into a window narrowly missing Walker. The bullet fragment was too mangled to be traced to any weapon. Whether Oswald did it, and whether he acted alone or with someone else, are open questions, but Marina told authorities that

Oswald admitted to her that he had shot at Walker.[163]

On April 21, Oswald dressed in a suit and placed a pistol in his pocket. He told Marina that former vice-president Richard Nixon was in town and hinted that he was going to try to find him. Horrified, Marina would not allow him to leave the house; at one point during the day she barricaded Lee in a bathroom until he promised not to go out.[164] At least, that is one of the stories she told; her testimony in the long run appears to have been full of inconsistencies and her credibility is subject to doubt.

Sometime during the same month a curious encounter between Dr. Adele Edisen and Dr. Jose Rivera eerily portended the fates of Oswald and Kennedy.[165] Edisen and Rivera met each other at a professional meeting in Washington D.C. Rivera introduced himself as a science administrator with the National Institute of Neurological Diseases, and made it clear that he had worked with hypnosis and LSD during his career. Edisen noted that Rivera was addressed by an acquaintance as Colonel Rivera. Polite conversation brought out the fact that Edisen lived in New Orleans, where Rivera had taught at Loyola University. Rivera mentioned knowing a Lee Harvey Oswald in New Orleans Edisen assumed that Oswald was a professional colleague. Curiously, within the same context, Rivera encouraged Edisen, whenever he might be in Dallas, to visit Jack Ruby's Carousel Club in Dallas.

Then Rivera asked Edisen to do him a favor: to contact Lee Oswald, whom he claimed to have taught at Loyola University. Rivera wanted to know when Oswald planned to leave New Orleans. He told Edisen to call Oswald and tell him to "kill the chief." Then Rivera cryptically added, without elaborating, that "we" are playing a joke on him. He also said that Oswald was not what he seemed, and that after "it's over" in November someone would kill Oswald. When Edisen asked for more details, Rivera refused.

Upon returning to New Orleans, Edisen called the phone number that Rivera had provided. First, he spoke to Marina Oswald, who claimed she did not know a Jose Rivera. Edisen called later and spoke to a man who identified himself as Lee Harvey Oswald; he also said he did not know Rivera. After the assassination, Edisen was determined to tell the FBI the full details of his strange encounter with "Colonel" Rivera. On November 24, 1963, he traveled to Washington to speak with agent Rice and gave him Rivera's phone number. Rice said nothing about Edisen's story other than to assure him that Rivera was harmless. The FBI has since told Edisen that they have no record of Edisen's meeting with Rice on November 24, 1963.[166]

FERRIE, CANCER, AND DR. SHERMAN

A medical treatise on cancer was found in Ferrie's apartment after his death. It has been speculated that Ferrie wrote the document, but recent research has questioned this theory. Ferrie was interested in cancer, but why he had such a fervent interest in the subject is unknown. Also in his apartment were laboratory mice that he supposedly used in experiments related to cancer. He had established a laboratory over his garage, where he claimed to have lost his hair due to experimentation with radiation, a chemical explosion, and cancer research experiments.[167]

Ed Haslam's book *Mary, Ferrie, and the Monkey Virus* investigates Ferrie's potential link to the mysterious murder of a brilliant orthopedic surgeon and cancer researcher Dr. Mary Sherman. Haslam believes that Sherman was involved in secret research into the possibility that polio vaccines were carcinogenic and would eventually cause cancer in those who were vaccinated. The vaccines were being promoted by the National Institute of Health, an organization of which Jose Rivera was a member. Haslam speculates that Sherman was engaged in research to find a way to counteract the carcinogenic effect of the vaccine, but she was stabbed to death and then her body was partially burned. Sherman's death has remained a mystery. Haslam writes that there is reason to believe that someone murdered Sherman, stole some of her papers, and tried to cover up the murder with a fire. The medical treatise on cancer that was found in Ferrie's apartment had no name associated with it, but it is Haslam's contention that an extremely knowledgeable person in the field wrote the paper in 1956, and not Ferrie.

Polio vaccines were in those days manufactured with polio viruses grown on the kidneys of monkeys. In 1959, Bernice Eddy found that cancer-causing monkey viruses had been found in the polio vaccines. When the NIH found out about Eddy's research, her professional career was finished. A US Congressional inquiry was made into Eddy's allegations, but nothing came of the investigation.[168]

Haslam reminds us of evidence that suggests that the AIDS virus is caused by a monkey virus that mutated sometime before 1969. Haslam speculates that this kind of virus could most probably have been created in a laboratory that benefited from a high level of medical knowledge, funding, and equipment — and was possibly intended for use as a biological weapon

MARCELLO, OSWALD, AND DEALEY PLAZA

During his public war on organized crime, Robert Kennedy, as attorney general, deported crime boss Carlos Marcello. On April 6, 1961 Marcello was whisked away in a plane and dumped on a Guatemalan beach. Two months later Marcello found his way back into the country, possibly piloted by David Ferrie.[169] Marcello vowed to get even.

In September 1962, private investigator Ed Becker met with Ferrie's boss, Carlos Marcello. He hoped to obtain funds from Marcello for an oil venture. During a whiskey-laced conversation at Marcello's country estate in Louisiana, Becker mentioned the deportation. Marcello angrily announced that Robert Kennedy "would be taken care of." However, he hinted that it would be done in a roundabout manner. He declared that to kill a dog, "you don't cut off the tail, but the head." The head would be the president, and the plan would include finding a nut to take the blame, "the way they do it in Sicily."[170]

On November 9–10 and 16–17, the two weekends prior to the assassination, Ferrie was working with Carlos Marcello at Marcello's remote farmhouse known as Churchill Farms. When asked about these meetings Ferrie told the FBI that they met to "map out a strategy for Marcello's trial," *The United States v. Carlos Marcello*. An FBI report of April 1961 indicated Marcello offered Sergio Arcacha Smith a deal whereby Marcello would make a substantial donation to his anti-

Castro movement in return for concessions in Cuba after Castro's ouster. Carlos Quiroga, the Cuban involved in the Cuban Revolutionary Front and seen at Mancuso's by David Lewis, said Ferrie lent Sergio Arcacha Smith money when he needed it for his family. This generosity occurred just after Ferrie lost his job with Eastern airlines.[171] On the day of the assassination Ferrie was in a courtroom with Carlos Marcello. Marcello was found innocent of all charges brought against him by Robert Kennedy.

Carlos Marcello

Jim Garrison, a friend of C. Wray Gill, decided to check the records of telephone calls made from Gill's office during November 1963. He found that the records were missing, and that Ferrie had had access to them. Gill told Garrison that Ferrie had made numerous long distance phone calls from Gill's office in 1962 and 1963. During questioning by New Orleans D.A. assistant Herman Kohlman and Secret Service Agent John Rice, Ferrie denied that he had been in Dallas in the past eight to ten years. However, a close investigation of Gill's phone records by Canadian researcher Peter Whitmey shows that Ferrie had made numerous phones calls from the Dallas and Fort Worth area.[172] Phone records show Ferrie called Dallas from New Orleans as late as August 10, 1963; called New Orleans from Fort Worth on September 10, 1963; and called New Orleans from Houston November 17, 1963 (a call that appeared on a December billing). Clearly, Ferrie had lied about his visits to Dallas.

Minutes after the assassination an investigation of the Dal-Tex Building, situated at Elm and Houston Streets overlooking Dealey Plaza, turned up a man named Eugene Brading. Brading had recently had his name changed to Jim Braden. An elevator man had noticed a suspicious person using the freight elevator, and he called the police. The police questioned Braden who said he had taken the elevator to the third floor to find a telephone. The police released Braden, not knowing his real identity. Eugene Brading was a convicted felon, a thief and embezzler with alleged ties to the supposedly Mafioso-related Smalldone family. Braden had stayed at the Cabana Motel in Dallas the night before. The Campisi brothers, Joe and Sam, who had close relationships with Jack Ruby and Carlos Marcello, owned the Cabana. Joe Campisi had played golf and visited the racetrack with the Marcello brothers on several occasions. In 1978, Campisi proudly told congressional investigators that he sent hundreds of pounds of sausage to Marcello each Christmas. Ruby had visited the Cabana's Egyptian Lounge the night before the shooting, had met with a Chicago businessman named Lawrence Meyers, and made several phone calls, some as late as 2:30 a.m. on the day of the assassination. Early on the day of the assassination, Braden had checked in with parole officers at a Dallas federal courthouse. He gave his New Orleans address as the same building and floor where David Ferrie kept an office. Despite many efforts to link Brading to a conspiracy, no one has succeeded in making a credible case. Brading testified in front of the House Select Committee on Assassinations, professing his innocence.

Other FBI investigations at this time focused on New Orleans. The more agents investigated Ferrie's life, the more links they found with Oswald. The relationship surely caused some suspicion in the FBI because they knew Ferrie had a verifiable relationship with Carlos Marcello.[173] Just when the investigation was yielding clearer links between all of these individuals, Director Hoover abruptly closed the it — on December 6, 1963, only two weeks after the assassination. None of the information the FBI collected concerning Ferrie was ever presented to the Warren Commission. David Belin, a former Warren Commission counsel, wrote a book in 1988, *Final Disclosure*, in which he defended the Warren Commission's findings that Oswald was the sole gunman. Belin never mentions David Ferrie.

On June 9, 1988, an FBI document (CR137A-5467-69) was released that outlined testimony from an unknown man concerning Marcello and his interest in the Kennedys. The document, which was heavily edited, read in part, "Marcello was talking about the

Kennedys. He told me and my friend about a meeting with Oswald. He had been introduced to Oswald by a man named Ferris [*sic* — a typo referring to Ferrie?], who was Marcello's pilot. He said that the [meeting] had taken place in his brother's restaurant [La Louisiane Restaurant] . . . He said that Ruby was a homo son of a bitch but good to have around to report to him what was happening in town . . . He flew into a rage . . . and said, 'Yea, I had the little son of a bitch killed, and I would do it again . . .' "[174]

WHISPERS OF PLOTS

On February 13, 1964, Canadian Richard Giesbrecht unwittingly overheard a conversation between two men in the Horizon Room of the Winnipeg International Airport. Giesbrecht noticed that one of the men had "the oddest hair and eyebrows I'd ever seen." Ferrie's companion was approximately the same age as him, late forties, wore a hearing aid and spoke with a Latin accent. Giesbrecht heard Ferrie tell his companion that he was concerned about how much Oswald had told his wife about the plot to kill Kennedy. They spoke of the Warren

Commission investigation and discussed a man called "Isaacs" and his relationship with Oswald, and wondered why he had gotten involved with someone so "psycho" as Oswald. One of the men lamented the fact that Isaacs had been caught on television film sometime during the Dallas motorcade. Ferrie said that "they" had more money than ever. Then Giesbrecht caught a snippet of a conversation relating to a meeting that was to take place in March in Missouri, since there had been no meeting since November of 1963. Giesbrecht immediately contacted the FBI, through his attorney. He gave details of the conversation, and after seeing a picture of Ferrie asserted that Ferrie was the man he had seen and heard at the Winnipeg airport. After questioning Giesbrecht and telling him that his information was important and was "the break we've been waiting for," the FBI contacted him several months later and told him to forget about the matter — because it was too serious. They cited the fact that he was a Canadian and there would be nothing the FBI could do for him if he needed protection. In a 1969 interview, Giesbrecht told writer Paris Flammonde that he was

100% certain the man he saw at the Winnipeg Airport was David Ferrie. Jim Garrison spoke to Giesbrecht about testifying at the Shaw trial. Giesbrecht claimed that he was threatened with harm to his family, and notified Garrison that he would not come to New Orleans and testify.[175]

The FBI interviewed two "Isaacs" who could possibly have a connection to the case. In March 1964, Martin Isaacs, a social worker in New York City, was interviewed about his involvement with the Oswalds when they first arrived in the US from Russia. They also interviewed Charles R. Isaacs, in January 1964, because his place of employment was listed in Jack Ruby's notebook. The FBI reports claim that Martin Isaacs had no knowledge of anything that had transpired at the Winnipeg Airport. The report on Charles Isaacs added little to the case, other than the fact that Mrs. Isaacs had worked for Ruby as a wardrobe designer.[176] Another Isaacs to consider is Harold R. Isaacs, supposedly an ex-*Newsweek* magazine editor who was the subject of a suppressed Warren commission document. Research conducted by Dick Russell found that Harold Isaacs was involved with leftist newspapers in Shanghai and knew Oswald's cousin Marilyn Murret. In 1963 he was a research associate at MIT. He was acquainted with Agnes Smedley, who was accused by "US Military Intelligence" of having "been a member of a Soviet spy ring."[177] Another source found ties between Isaacs and CIA agent Gary Underhill, who was apparently murdered when he threatened to expose US intelligence agencies as the source of the assassination.[178] However, the source of the Underhill information is documented only through the highly controversial work of William Torbitt (a pseudonym for a Texas lawyer David Copeland), whose *Nomenclature of an Assassination Cabal* (aka The Torbitt Document) is a book-length study of the assassination focusing on numerous clandestine organizations allegedly involved in the assassination.[179] It is supported by questionable documentation.[180] No one has firmly tied Oswald with any "Isaacs" or any communist spy ring.

In November 1993, a woman contacted Peter Whitmey and told him that on November 18 or 19 of 1963 she went to the Winnipeg Airport to retrieve a package. While waiting in the Horizon Room, she overheard a conversation between three men. One of them said that someone was going to be killed in Dallas that coming Friday. She never told any authorities about what she heard and claims that she never knew about Giesbrecht's similar experience in February of 1964.[181]

In February 2003, Dick Russell documented a similar story concerning Ferrie and another overheard conversation concerning a plot against the president. Art Escarze, a Cuban exile who once served as a bodyguard for the Cuban exile leader Antonio de Varona, told Russell he worked against Castro's regime for the CIA in the Sixties. In one mission, Escarze and associates investigated a group of seven men in New Orleans in the summer of 1963. At a restaurant, Escarze observed three men who wore Cuban military dress, and one man who was remarkably ugly, " …lot of red hair, and he walked funny. I don't know if he was gay or not. But I heard his name. They called him Mr. Ferrie." Escarze later identified another young man ("normal looking, short hair") as

Oswald. Escarze heard the group talking about killing Kennedy; Oswald was to shoot and draw attention while "two other people would also be shooting," and then someone was saying that the best place to do it would be " ... where there is a lot of people." Escarze wrote a report on the incident and turned it in to a CIA contact. Russell showed Escarze a photograph of Richard Nagell but Escarze could not identify him as one in the group. Escarze believes that the plotters were working for Castro but Russell points out that the CIA could easily have set up such a bizarre encounter, possibly in the hopes of linking Castro to a plot after the assassination. "Could it have been more obvious?" writes Russell. "Three men in Cuban military garb . . . bringing up Castro's name . . . being overheard. Escarze's crew, already fervently anti-Castro, would have been only too pleased to fall victim to such a ploy."[182]

FERRIE THE SUSPECT

In February of 1967, New Orleans D.A. Jim Garrison announced that he was reopening the investigation into the president's assassination. Garrison's announcement came the day after John Roselli, a Mafia figure with ties to various mafioso bosses throughout the country, told Chief Justice Earl Warren through his attorney that he had been involved in several CIA attempts to assassinate Fidel Castro. Roselli claimed that in retaliation Castro's agents, in conjunction with the Mafia, planned the murder of the president.

In February 1967, Garrison announced that David Ferrie was one of his chief suspects. He placed him in protective custody, accompanied by a bodyguard, in a New Orleans hotel. Ferrie publicly scoffed at Garrison's allegations, telling journalists that "I have been pegged as the getaway pilot in an elaborate plot to kill Kennedy" and that it was "fruitless to look for an accomplice of Oswald." On February 12, 1968, Garrison accused Oswald's Marine acquaintance, Kerry Thornley, of perjuring himself in testimony concerning the assassination. Thornley, author of the novel *The Idle Warriors*, had based his main character on Oswald. Garrison read the novel and claimed that Thornley was part of a plot to create a false impression of Oswald, which was designed to frame him for the murder. Thornley, in his 1991 reprint of *The Idle Warriors*, claimed he had met Clay Shaw, Guy Banister, David Ferrie, and possibly Gordon Novel, all before November 22, 1963. Thornley is not clear on the specifics of why he met the men but hints that the meetings were innocent and coincidental.[183]

In 1995, Lou Ivon, an investigator for Garrison told JFK researcher William Davy that he had spoken to Ferrie on February 18, 1967 while he was in protective custody in the Fountainbleau Hotel in New Orleans. Ferrie had complained to Garrison and his investigators that he feared for his life. Ferrie told Ivon that he had been a contract employee of the CIA, he knew Shaw and Oswald, and he hated Kennedy.[184] Ferrie went as far as to say that he, Oswald, Banister, and Shaw all worked for the CIA.[185] On February 21, Ferrie was inexplicably released from protective custody before he had completed his testimony; he returned to his apartment.

Ferrie was found dead the next day. Two typed notes were left that suggested suicide. The first began, "To leave this life, to me, is a sweet prospect." For several paragraphs he rambled on about crime in

America and the incompetence of the American government. The second note was brief and declared that, "when you read this I will be quite dead and no answer will be possible." New Orleans Metro Crime Commission director, Aaron Kohn, believed that Ferrie had been murdered. The New Orleans coroner officially reported that the cause of death was natural: a cerebral hemorrhage. The coroner officially listed the death as due to "rupture of berry aneurysm circle of Willis south massive left subdural hematoma and subarachnoid hemorrhage, and secondary pontine hemorrhages." In Ferrie's final interview with journalist George Lardner in the early morning hours of February 22, 1967, he denied knowing Oswald or traveling to Cuba at any time.[186]

During his investigation, Garrison found that before the assassination Ferrie had deposited over $7,000 in his bank account, and after the assassination someone purchased Ferrie a gasoline-station franchise. Ferrie also secured a job with Marcello-based United Air Taxi Corporation and later worked for a few years for Marcello associate Jacob Nastasi's air cargo service firm. Marcello testified that he paid Ferrie $7,000 for Ferrie's paralegal work in November of 1963. Though Ferrie had several interesting connections to the assassination, Garrison never linked any of Ferrie's activities to Marcello.[187]

## SHAW, FERRIE, AND OSWALD

The House Select Committee investigated reports of Oswald being seen in Clinton, Louisiana in August-September of 1963. These reports were not available to the Warren Commission, though one witness (Reeves Morgan) said he notified the FBI when he recognized Oswald from news photographs right after the assassination. Gerald Posner claims there is no record of such a call. Garrison was the first to bring the Clinton sightings to the public in 1967. The synthesis of the testimony of six witnesses contributed to an account that placed Oswald in "Jackson, La., seeking employment at East Louisiana State Hospital . . . on advice that his job would depend on his becoming a registered voter, Oswald went to Clinton for that purpose . . . he referred to himself as 'Oswald,' and he produced his Marine Corps discharge papers as identification. Some of the witnesses said that Oswald was accompanied by two older men whom they identified as Ferrie and Shaw." [188]

Several witnesses recognized Shaw as the driver of a limousine with Ferrie, who wore a rumpled wig and painted eyebrows, sitting next to Shaw and Oswald in the back. Witness Corey Collins stated in an affidavit that he identified Clay Shaw as the man "who was sitting behind the wheel of a black Cadillac," the same car that held "Lee Harvey Oswald and David Ferrie." Collins testified in court that Shaw was the man he saw in the car. However, it is also possible that Banister may have been the elderly, white-haired driver. Banister suspected that CORE (Congress on Racial Equality), the organization that arranged the voter registration, was a Communist strategy established to destroy the US.[189] Having an admitted Communist like Oswald as part of the registration may have been part of a plot to infiltrate and discredit CORE, an opinion shared by researchers Anthony Summers and Philip Melanson. Some investigators, like Gerald Posner and Armand Moss[190] have questioned the plot to discredit CORE.

Posner mentions that Garrison's investigators interviewed more than 300 people in Clinton and neighboring Jackson, an amazing 20 percent of the entire local population. Only six witnesses were produced. The initial statements of these witnesses, according to Posner, were confused and only after coaching was Garrison's staff able to produce a consistent story. Posner also questions the timing of the visit. He questions that the visit was before September 24, the date Oswald left New Orleans for good; but this is based only on a comment by Ed McGehee, the Jackson town barber, who claimed to have cut Oswald's hair when the temperature was cool. One witness, Jim Alcock, was sure that the visit occurred in late August or early September, clearly before the September 24 cut-off date. The registrar of voters, Henry Palmer, testified at the Garrison trial that a man attempted to register to vote using a US Navy ID card with the name of Lee H. Oswald and a New Orleans address, a fact that Posner recognizes.

Why would Oswald be seeking employment at East Louisiana State Hospital[191] in Jackson, Louisiana? A theory set forth by Jean Davison, author of *Oswald's Game*, focuses on the possibility that Banister and/or Ferrie were seeking psychiatric records for a client (Smith? Marcello?). Even if Ferrie knew very little about Oswald, he would deny knowing him if Oswald were asked to illegally obtain mental health records. Davison proposes an interesting theory based on the fact that an expensive miniature hi-tech Minox "spy" camera[192] was found in Oswald's personal effects at the Paine house.

Years before, in April 1953, the CIA had begun research in mind control with the authorization of director Allen Dulles. Proposed by Richard Helms and managed by Dr. Sidney Gottlieb, the project was given the name of MK-ULTRA and eventually went beyond mind control into the development of deadly toxins. Marrs asserts that one of two CIA field stations involved with MK-ULTRA was in Atsugi, Japan, where Oswald served as a Marine radar operator and has been alleged to have been involved in undercover operations. The station held large quantities of LSD and other mind-altering substances.[193]

Shaw and Ferrie's relationships with leaders of right-wing organizations like the Ku

Klux Klan, John Birch Society, The Constitution Party, and the Minutemen[194] have led to speculation by William Holden that the meeting of these men in Clinton was a calculated right-wing scheme to link Oswald and his "legend" as a communist sympathizer with "the Civil Rights Movement and perhaps other leftist groups ... such as the American Civil Liberties, Fair Play for Cuba Committee and possibly the New Orleans Committee for Peaceful Alternatives."[195] Shaw's superior at the Trade Mart was Lloyd Cobb, a wealthy right-wing extremist, whose brother Alvin was a KKK member. Alvin Cobb has been linked to Banister.[196] Ferrie was twice seen at Lakefront Airport in New Orleans with California Minuteman Eugene Bradley.[197] After Ruby's arrest in the killing of Oswald, a white envelope with the phone number of Robert Welch, founder of the John Birch Society, was found in Ruby's clothes.[198] Ferrie told Julian Buznedo, an associate of Sergio Arcacha Smith, that he was "working with some wealthy people from the John Birch Society who are helping at the refugee camps."[199] Ruby was carrying $7,000 three hours after the assassination and had $2,000 on him after his arrest. An additional $10,000 was found in the trunk of his car.[200]

RIGHT-WING FOREKNOWLEDGE?

A right-wing association with the assassination takes on more significance in consideration of the comments of Joseph Milteer and the actions of H.L. Hunt. Milteer, a wealthy Georgian and leader of a right-wing organization called National States Rights Party. An FBI informer taped a conversation on November 9, 1963, in which Milteer spoke of an assassination plot to kill Kennedy from a window with a high-powered rifle.[201] After the assassination Milteer described himself as part of an "international underground" that used Oswald as a dupe to put blame on the Communists. Dick Russell (*The Man Who Knew Too Much*) wonders how H.L. Hunt fits in. He cites the following: H.L. Hunt funded American paramilitary and East European émigré groups; the previously mentioned "Dear Mr. Hunt" letter; visits of Jack Ruby and Eugene Brading to Hunt's office shortly before the assassination; two former employees of Hunt who alleged that the Hunts purchased the original copy of the

Zapruder film; a Hunt employee who was sent to Dallas to check security surrounding Oswald the night before he was shot; Jack Ruby drove an employee to the Hunt offices sometime around November 20, 1963; H.L. Hunt received a visit from Marina Oswald after the assassination.[202]

*The Man Who Knew Too Much*, Dick Russell

On November 23, 1963, the day after the assassination, Milteer told Somersett that there was a communist conspiracy by Jews to overthrow the United States. On November 24, he supposedly made a speech at Columbia, South Carolina where he declared to Christians that the Jews had killed Christ and Kennedy, and now his organization was going to kill Jews. Milteer has been described as an Evangelical Christian who believed that the Jews were needed to establish a Jewish state, because only after that would Jesus return to earth. (The world would end with most of the Jews killed and only a few survivors converting to Christianity.)

RUBY AND FERRIE

On September 24, 1963, Ferrie allegedly made a phone call to a Chicago apartment building where Jean West (aka Jean Aase) resided. Whether the phone call was received by Ms. West is unknown, to this day. Ms. West had been at the Cabana Motel with Lawrence Meyers on the night of the assassination, along with Jack Ruby, who left early to return to his club to count the night's receipts. The Cabana Motel was the same place where Eugene Brading had stayed. Investigator Peter Whitmey interviewed Ms. West in 1993. He reported that she claimed that the fifteen-minute phone call on September 24, 1963 was between Ferrie and Meyers but in a follow-up interview in 1998 with Whitmey, West asserted that she had not known Meyers until a few weeks before the assassination.[203] Meyers testified in front of the House Select Committee on Assassinations that he never knew Ferrie; and

Jean West never testified. Whitmey also discovered that Ferrie had made phone calls from Dallas on January 21 and 29, 1963, though the significance of these calls has never been understood — other than proving that Ferrie lied to the Secret Service when he told them he had not been in Dallas for "eight to ten years."[204] Garrison and numerous other investigators have found the Chicago phone call suspicious; but despite more thorough investigation of the phone call, no significance has been found for the links between West, Ruby, Meyers, and Brading.[205] Though there may not be any important connection between the owners and visitors to the Cabana Motel on November 21, 1963, it remains a strange coincidence that Mafioso-linked Eugene Brading stayed at the motel owned by the Campisi brothers, who had significant relationships with Ruby and Carlos Marcello. Additionally, Marcello had a significant relationship with David Ferrie, who may have made a phone call to Lawrence Meyers, another customer of the Cabana that night.

Ferrie was known to use an alias of "Ferris" on occasions. The Warren

Commission reported the fact that Jack Ruby's address book contained the name of "Ferris."[206] No other link between Ferrie and Ruby has ever been conclusively established. Beverly Oliver, in her book *Nightmare in Dallas*, wrote that Ferrie was a visitor to the Carousel Club in 1963. She describes Ferrie as a shifty-eyed, creepy-looking man who could speak several languages and engaged in a boasting match with Ruby. She also maintains that Ferrie offered $50,000 to Larry Ronco, Oliver's friend and fellow employee at the Carousel, to kill Castro. Ms. Oliver, mistakenly identified as the "Babushka Lady"[207] of Dealey Plaza, makes other assertions, which include seeing Oswald at the Carousel, seeing Roscoe White on the grassy knoll immediately after the shooting, and having her film of the assassination confiscated by FBI agents, never to be returned. The HSCA wrote that Oliver's story was troubling but contained several contradictions of established fact. Sam and Chuck Giancana's book *Double Cross*, which is accorded little respect in the research community, makes an unsubstantiated claim that Ruby hired Ferrie at his Carousel Club in

Dallas. Oliver's lack of credibility is only matched by Judyth Vary Baker who claims she was Oswald's mistress during his brief stay in New Orleans in 1963, an assertion that has been rejected by numerous researchers and major network news organizations.[208]

HYPNOSIS AND THE ASSASSIN OF THE SIXTIES

On December 2, 1963, Gene Barnes, an NBC cameraman, made the following statement to the FBI: "Barnes said Bob Mulholland, NBC News, Chicago, talked in Dallas to one Fairy, [*sic*] a narcotics addict now out on bail on a sodomy charge in Dallas. Fairy said that Oswald had been under hypnosis from a man doing a mind-reading act at Ruby's 'Carousel.' Fairy was said to be a private investigator and the owner of an airplane who took young boys on flights 'just for kicks.'"[209] Mulholland later said that he had been quoted incorrectly and that he had heard FBI agents mention Ferrie's name as a possible link to Oswald. [210] Mind control and hypnosis have appeared several times in conjunction with Oswald.

Along with Mulholland's story, Jack Martin and Richard Nagell[211] claim that Ferrie hypnotized Oswald; Landry was hypnotized by Ferrie; the mysterious Rivera who casually mentioned his expertise of hypnosis in the same conversation mentioning Oswald; and J. Edgar Hoover's testimony to the Warren Commission that "information came to me indicating that there is an espionage training school outside Minsk — I don't know whether it is true — and that Oswald was trained at that school to come back to this country to become what they call a 'sleeper,' . . . a man who will remain dormant for three or four years and in case of international hostilities rise up and be used."[212] The 1967 book *Were We Controlled?* explored the possibility that Oswald had been implanted with electronic devices designed to aid in mind control. Oswald did have an operation in Minsk at the end of March of 1961.[213]

Martin Luther King's accused assassin, James Earl Ray, was also interested in hypnosis. When he was arrested in London, his bags contained the book *Self-Hypnotism: The Technique and Its Use in Daily Living*. Four months before King was shot, Ray met with Reverend Xavier von Koss, the head of the International Society of Hypnosis in Los Angeles. Koss tested Ray for susceptibility to hypnosis but claimed he "quickly encountered very strong subconscious resistance." Robert Kennedy's assassin Sirhan Sirhan told authorities he did not remember shooting him. A psychiatrist hired by Sirhan's defense attorney, Dr. Bernard Diamond, was convinced that Sirhan had prior experience with hypnosis. Sirhan told biographer Robert Blair Kaiser that he had visited the Philosophical Research Center of Manley Palmer Hill, a hypnosis research center in southern California. Sirhan repetitively wrote in his diary, "RFK must die" followed by "practice, practice, practice, practice, practice, practice, Mind Control, Mind Control, Mind Control."[214] Sheikh Omar Abdul Rahman, the mastermind of the first World Trade Center bombing, has been quoted as telling one of his confederates to "slowdown" in his eagerness to plan several bombings in New York in 1993. "The one who killed Kennedy [Sirhan?] was trained for three years," he told follower Emad Salem.[215] In March 1973, Black September terrorists seized the Saudi Arabian Embassy in Khartoum, Sudan and demanded the release of Sirhan, sixty Palestinian guerrillas from Jordanian jails and Baader-

Meinhof Gang members jailed in West Germany. (No one was released.)

Though Oswald's motive for assassinating Kennedy may remain forever a mystery, it has been speculated that film and fiction stories he may have seen or read could have added to his motivation or incentive. He checked out of a Dallas library the book *From Russia with Love*; the plot features a psychotic killer who defected to Russia and became a state-sponsored assassin. John Luken has produced a complete study on the films, their connections, and their plots that could have been possible influences.[216] Luken introduces the strong possibility that Oswald saw *The Manchurian Candidate* and *We Were Strangers*, in which political assassins are the primary characters; *We Were Strangers* (1949) depicts a heroic American assassin trying to aid the Cuban people. Luken makes a powerful argument that these films could have been an influence in Oswald's actions. Luken also makes a strong case that Oswald saw *We Were Strangers* twice and identified with the leftist martyr hero. He may also have identified with Lawrence Harvey's character in *The Manchurian Candidate*, (1962) who was an army veteran returned to the US from behind enemy lines in the Korean War. The brainwashed veteran is controlled by his mother to kill a liberal politician. These films were shown in theaters and on television when Oswald had recently returned from the Soviet Union, where he had become disenchanted with the Russian life.

THE FRENCH CONNECTIONS

Stephen J. Rivelle examined a possible connection between the Corsican Mafia and the assassination. Rivelle's findings pointed to a Mafia hit called into Marseille, France by Carlos Marcello and possibly other American Mafia figures. To hide the trail, according to Rivelle, three French hitmen were used in the murder.[217]

The CIA knew within hours of the event that a French assassin was in Dallas on the day of the assassination; but this fact was never brought to the attention of the Warren Commission nor has it been fully investigated by scholars. A CIA document (632-796, located by researcher Mary Farrell) shows that unspecified US Judicial Department officials, for unspecified reasons, expelled a "Jean Souetre aka Michel Roux or Michel Mertz" from the United States sometime on November 24. The document states that Souetre was in Fort Worth the morning of November 22 (as was JFK) and in Dallas during the afternoon and he was expelled to either Mexico of Canada.[218] Jean Rene Souetre was a deserter of the French Army and an activist in the French OAS (*Organisation de l'Armee Secrete*). OAS has been described as a right-wing extremist group that opposes President Charles de Gaulle's granting Algeria independence from French rule. The OAS has a reputation for terror acts (including an assassination attempt on Jean Paul Sartre in 1961) and links to the French Mafia, especially organized crime in the Marseille area. However, authors O'Leary and Seymour

(*Triangle of Death*) believe that a Michel Mertz was using Souetre's name as a cover. Interviews by US officials and other journalists seem to have cleared Souetre, who claims that Michel Mertz, another shadowy figure supposedly ten years older than Souetre and involved in Mafia activity in France, was using Souetre's name in order to create an apparent link to the assassination. It is not at all clear who the Souetre, Mertz, or Roux referred to in the CIA report really are, which means that these leads are, once again, unresolvable dead-ends. The Russians, who had every reason to try to clear Oswald of any connection to the assassination, lest they be implicated, lent credence to the "French" and Mafia theory. Colonel Pavlotsy, the highest ranking officer in the KGB's investigative unit, said in an interview that a KGB investigation showed that Kennedy was killed by a hit team of French and South Vietnamese agents. "Our group found that the Corsicans hired French hitman Michel Mertz, sometimes known as Jean Rene Souetre, to carry out the assassination with the cooperation of the American Mafia bosses."[219]

*Farewell America — The Plot to Kill JFK,* one of many mysterious studies of the assassination the innumerable conspiracy theories around it, looks like a deliberate piece of disinformation. The original publisher has admitted that the author "James Hepburn" was fictitious and the true authors were in part French intelligence sources; Andre Ducret (DeGaulle's Secret Service director); Interpol; and Phillippe Vasjoly, a French petroleum agent for the United States. Printed in 1968, in several languages, this work was allegedly suppressed from wide circulation in the United States with the help of Hoover's FBI. The book incriminates a conglomeration of conspirators called "The Committee"; this group collectively comprised a host of Kennedy haters that included the usual roll call: the CIA, anti-Cuban mercenaries, and right-wing oil industry leaders. The Committee, they say, planned every aspect of the assassination, hiring four gunmen, and getting Oswald hired at the book depository and set up as a fall guy. Whether Oswald was a patsy, as he claimed, or not, *Farewell America* asserts that Ferrie, as a right-wing Minuteman and CIA agent, was expected to help set up

Oswald as a patsy while a real CIA Minuteman commando actually did the killing. "Oswald was probably told that he had been chosen to participate in a new anti-communist operation together with Ferrie and several other agents." Oswald would be led to believe that the attack was designed to influence public opinion against the Communists. How much Oswald knew is never clearly presented nor why he would be party to a scheme that left him, after the assassination, walking alone in the suburbs of Dallas with just a few dollars in his wallet.[220]

LOOKING BACK

Where does Oswald fit in the world of assassins? Like Princip, his real motives are a mystery — maybe they were a mystery to himself. The Warren Commission declared him a "lone nut," though assassins historically have had some motive whether they were the treacherous senators in Caesar's times, Booth, or even the self-proclaimed "anarchist" Leon Czolgosz, assassin of US President McKinley. Czolgosz was inspired by the assassination of Italy's King Humbert I by an anarchist. Princip was inspired by the failed Serbian assassin Bogdan Zerajic and was supported by the Serbian radical organization The Black Hand. Did Oswald draw inspiration and support from any creed or organization, and if so, which one(s)?

Ferrie was associated with a number of anti-Kennedy figures and men directly investigated in the assassination: Oswald, Shaw, Marcello, Smith, Banister, and anti-Castro figures, all of whom had different possible motives for harming the president. Ferrie contradicted himself about his relationship with Oswald and there is solid evidence that Ferrie lied about knowing Shaw. Strangely, he admitted to Lou Ivon, only days before his death, that he was acquainted with Oswald, Shaw, and Banister and that all were working with the CIA. He was photographed with Oswald and was seen with Oswald on more than one occasion by numerous witnesses. Then, in his last interview, only hours before his death, Ferrie denied that he knew Oswald. It is a similar story with Shaw: Ferrie was supposedly photographed more than once with Shaw, and was seen with Shaw on several occasions, though Ferrie and Shaw both denied any relationship. Ferrie worked directly with Marcello and Banister. Both

Marcello and Banister have been quoted at least once saying that they wished to get rid of the president in a violent manner, a threat that also has been attributed to Ferrie more than once. Ferrie was associated with Sergio Arcacha Smith, who was identified as a figure who may have been plotting the death of the president. Ferrie also lied about being in Dallas in 1963, and the accuracy of his comment to journalist Lardner that he had never been in Cuba can also be questioned. His actions directly after the assassination are bizarre: a frantic and inexplicable trip to a Houston ice rink where he spent hours on a pay phone. Other associations like Ruby are puzzling, though Ruby and Ferrie had a common acquaintance in Lawrence Meyers, and Ruby's address book contained the word "Ferris," possibly linking him with Ferrie.

In Ferrie's defense, many questions exist concerning the methods used by individuals who have presented information about him and others. Testimonies from Bundy, Beauboeuf, Russo, Lemanns, among others were established by means of hypnosis, sodium pentothal, and possibly bribery (and threats). It is very clear that either Garrison's investigators were using bribery to elicit testimony, or someone (the CIA plants mentioned by Marchetti?) was trying to make it appear that they were.

No material evidence proves that Ferrie was involved with any aspect of the assassination and in fact many such accusations have been found to be false. However, his personal and professional associations, and his history of clandestine activity, will always make him suspicious. The HSCA concluded that the Oswald-Ferrie relationship was significant.[221] Is it possible that David Ferrie could have associations with pro-Castro and anti-Castro groups, Communists and right-wing associations, the CIA, FBI, and the Mafia, and a seemingly endless number of others, let alone the officially recognized assassin Oswald, and have nothing to do with the death of Kennedy, a man whom he despised?

\*

Decades of investigating the JFK assassination has both enlightened the American public on what happened in Dealey Plaza as well as question the American government's role in clearly resolving some of the key questions to the murder. Unlike previous American presidential assassins, the prime suspect of JFK's death never admitted his role in the killing and never had a chance for a trial. Oswald's motivation will forever be clouded in mystery and likely misunderstanding. Unlike another twentieth-century, limousine-shooting assassin Gavrilo Princip who clearly stated a reason for his action, Oswald never admitted to anything in the few hours he lived after the assassination.

Though numerous writers have sought to weave a conspiratorial tone into Oswald's actions that day, years of investigation have provided some telling facts as to what happened mid-day in Dallas, Texas: Oswald owned the murder weapon, a fiber of the shirt he wore that day was found wedged within a crevice of his rifle found on the sixth floor of the Texas School Book Depository,[222] his fingerprints and palm prints were found on boxes in the sniper's nest, the only bullet fragments found in the presidential limousine were linked directly to Oswald's rifle, an eyewitness to the shooting identified Oswald as the man that shot a rifle from the sixth floor's sniper's nest, Oswald fled quickly from the scene of the shooting, 45-minutes later Oswald shot Officer J.D. Tippit with the same pistol found in his possession when apprehended, Oswald pulled the same pistol on Officer MacDonald when being apprehended at the Texas Theater, Oswald lied numerous times concerning various aspects of the assassination to Dallas police and U.S. government authorities during his interrogation to demonstrate what assassination investigator and author Vincent Bugliosi characterized as " . . . showing a consciousness of guilt."[223] Without a trial, tales of conspiracy have flown around the case for decades and likely decades more.[224] Though a second or more shooters in Dealey Plaza has been investigated like few other mysteries in the world, the fact that Oswald acted alone in the plaza remains the prevailing theory.

*Reclaiming History – The Assassination of President John F. Kennedy*, Vincent Bugliosi

Bugliosi said of Oswald's guilt and motivation, " . . . everything pointed toward Oswald's guilt. All the physical evidence, all the scientific evidence. Everything he said, everything he did. In *Reclaiming History*, at the end of book one, I set forth 53 separate pieces of evidence pointing toward Oswald's guilt. It would not be humanly possible for this man to be innocent and still have 53 pieces of evidence pointing toward his guilt. Only in a fantasy world can you have 53 pieces of evidence pointing toward guilt and still be innocent. Quickly, five pieces: Oswald's Mannlicher-Carcano rifle was the murder weapon. That's pretty heavy by itself. Oswald was the only employee at the Book Depository Building who fled the building after the assassination. Forty-five minutes later, he shoots and kills Officer J. D. Tippit, Dallas Police Department. That murder bore the signature of a man in desperate flight from some awful deed. Thirty minutes later at a Texas theatre he resists arrest, pulls a gun on the arresting officer. During his interrogation, [Oswald] told one provable lie after another, showing a consciousness of guilt . . . no one is ever going to know for sure why Oswald killed Kennedy. Even if he were alive today, *he might not be able to tell us* the dynamics swirling around in his fevered mind that led him to this monstrous act of murder." [225]

Where Princip wanted to further the cause of Apis's Black Hand through his group of the Young Bosnians, or John W. Booth wanted to avenge the Southern cause in his killing of Lincoln, Oswald might have wanted to further the cause of the 1960s Castro Cuban Revolution by using his rifle against General Walker and JFK. He revered Castro and once commented to a friend that he wanted to train Cuban soldiers. He had begged his wife Marina to help him hijack an airplane to Cuba. He blatantly associated himself with various pro and anti-Castro people in hopes that his "legend" as a Cold War warrior would bring him a meaningful life in Cuba; to the last moment of his life he had suffered numerous personal failings. Authors Bugliosi (*Reclaiming History*), Epstein (*Legend*), Mailer (*Oswald's Tale*) and others have delved into the troubled mind of Oswald only to describe a disturbing portrait with too many puzzle pieces missing to fully understand a complete and verifiable motive to his bizarre and troubling actions before and after Dealey Plaza. Subsequent investigations into the assassination like the Warren Commission and the HSCA have left much of the American public with an uneasy feeling toward their own government's interest in the truth. Hundreds of books and articles on the assassination have clouded the reality of the act with vast conspiracies rooted in conspiratorial fantasies of a magic bullet, mystery shooters behind fences, ice bullets, umbrella guns, subterranean gunmen ensconced within Elm Street sewer drains as well as phantom assassins within the Texas School Book Depository whose only aim was to kill JFK, escape undetected, and frame Oswald.

*Oswald's Tale – An American Mystery*, Norman Mailer

In August of 1963, Oswald had been filmed handing out Fair Play for Cuba leaflets on New Orleans streets. The Fair Play for Cuba organization was as strange and lonely in the world as its only member – Lee H. Oswald. Like Russia, Oswald had an early interest in Cuba and had talked about his desire to help the revolution by training Castro's troops, a declaration he made while in the Marines.[226] He was so desperate to get to Cuba that he proposed that he and Marina hijack a plane out of New Orleans to Cuba, a plan that Marina rejected immediately.[227]

He was proud that he could do things on his own without any complications or expense. He told Marina he was amused that people thought some kind of grand plan had to be devised for someone to shoot at General Edwin Walker and escape without notice. He had used no accomplices in the Walker shooting, and had likely transported his Mannlicher-Carcano by wrapping it in a blanket and taking it on a bus to the shooting. He hid the rifle and returned for it days later. He scoffed at the next morning's newspaper that got his story wrong. He said to Marina, "They say I had a .30 caliber bullet when I didn't at all . . . they got the bullet and the rifle all wrong . . . what fools."[228] Whatever the obstacles were in the Walker case, Oswald was able to execute the attempted assassination of Walker with his cheap rifle, escape unnoticed with nothing more expensive than bus fare, hide the rifle, and return the weapon back to his own safekeeping.

Oswald traveled to Mexico City in September of 1963.[229] Though the exact reason for going to Mexico City is unknown, it is likely he was seeking a visa. He made several documented visits to both the Russian and Cuban Embassies asking for a visa. Oswald's interest in Cuba and its Castro-led regime has played a major role in spinning conspiracy theories involving Oswald, Castro, and the Cuban intelligence service, DGI [*Directorio General de Inteligencia*].

During one of his emotional September 1963 visits to the Mexico City Russian Embassy, a distraught Oswald pleaded with the Russians for a visa and allegedly produced his A. Hidell .38 snub-nosed pistol claiming he had to carry it to safeguard himself from people who were following him.[230] At the same time, Oswald has been associated with making verbal threats to Kennedy while being in Mexico City, a fact that cannot be verified.[231] There are no reliable sources for Oswald making threats to President Kennedy before the assassination though the subject continues to appear in studies and books decades after the incident.[232]

With the cold rejection of the Mexico City embassies still in mind, did Oswald believe he had to prove himself beyond his Fair Play for Cuba credentials? If he was able to boast of killing or injuring Walker, he would have made the argument that he was worthy of becoming a citizen of Castro's revolutionary Cuba. Did he dream through October and November of 1963 of returning to the embassies with proof that he was a radical Cuban revolutionary worthy of acceptance into Castro's island? Rejection and failure was his constant companion. He had failed in his attempt to assassinate Edwin Walker and coldly denied visas to Cuba and Russia. His wife had rejected his idea of hijacking a plane to Cuba and scoffed at the idea. Was he left with only one option: his trusted rifle and the violent statement it could affirm of his desire to be a Cuban? Was he determined to seek out another opportunity to exercise his rifle in his personal revolution?

On September 26, 1963 JFK mentioned in an interview that he would visit Texas, and it was reported by the *Dallas Morning News*. On November 18, 1963 JFK made a speech in Miami to the Inter-American Press Association where he encouraged Cubans to rebel against Castro. On November 19, the *Dallas Morning News* wrote that the President's motorcade would travel from Love Field along "Harwood to Main, Main to Houston, Houston to Elm, Elm under the Triple Underpass to Stemmons Freeway, and on to the Trade Mart." On November 21st, Oswald visited the Paine's house in Irving, Texas where Marina Oswald and her two children were temporarily living and stayed the night. He begged Marina three times to join him again, but he was rejected. Marina later said she refused to be threatened by him citing previous abuse at his hand and could not agree to live with him until his behavior had changed. On the morning of November 22, he left most of his money and his wedding ring on a bedroom bureau. He secretly retrieved his rifle from the garage where it had been stored and wrapped it in shipping paper. He hitched a ride with coworker Wes Frazier to the Texas School Book Depository in Dealey Plaza with his deadly package in hand and thirteen dollars in his wallet.

From his infamous $6^{th}$-floor sniper's nest within the Texas School Book Depository, Oswald considered his options for shooting angles and opportunities. His shadowy figure was seen by numerous people on the street below before and during the shooting. He was seen by one witness looking down Elm Street toward the triple underpass where the motorcade would exit Dealey Plaza. By shooting down Elm Street when the presidential limousine had passed him, he would avoid the eyes of the Secret Servicemen following the limousine. He could see an opening shot between the traffic signal and the oak tree. The shot would theoretically hit the back or side of the president while the Secret Service car faced away from the sniper's nest pointed down Elm Street. While the limousine moved under the oak tree branches, the rifle could be reloaded and sighted for a second, third, or fourth shot that would be clear from the tree to the underpass.

President Kennedy, wife Jacqueline, Gov. John Connally, wife Nellie in presidential limousine, November 22, 1963, Dallas, Texas U.S.A.

He had loaded his rifle with a Mannlicher clip containing four cartridges. The clip could hold six cartridges. Three shells were found in the sniper's nest. The fourth cartridge was loaded in the rifle and extracted by police when the rifle was found on the sixth floor hidden between boxes.

As the limousine and Secret Service follow-up car turned onto Elm Street at approximately 12:30 p.m., Oswald pointed his rifle toward Elm Street at an acute 45-30 degree downward angle over the limousine that slowed to turn from Houston to Elm directly below the sniper's nest. Though this was the closest shot (as close as 97 feet) he could execute without the likely eyes of the

Secret Service seeing him, he was in an awkward position of either kneeling or crouching behind his support boxes with the window only half open. He fired the rifle that created a strange firecracker or backfire sound to the earwitnesses on the street. The sound of the rifle was muted by the fact that the rifle was withdrawn partially within the building. This sound would be different from the next two shots he took as he tracked the limousine farther down Elm and positioned his rifle at a drastically different angle and position within the window. Though he had a scope to aid in his aim, he might have simply used the sights on the rifle instead of the scope.

    The first shot missed. It did not hit anyone in the limousine or the limousine. Governor Connally heard the first shot and turned to his left. He recognized it as a rifle shot. Oswald's shot either hit an obstruction (the traffic signal, the metal traffic signal arm that stretched over Elm Street from north to south, or a tree branch), *or* the shot was fired before he was able to establish an accurate aim in which the shot missed the limousine completely and hit the street with such force that it completely disintegrated without any trace of copper or lead to examine. Witnesses saw "smoke" and "dust" fly up from the street close to the limousine before the second and third shots were fired.

Oswald quickly pulled the bolt on his rifle to reload. He saw the motorcade moving slowly down Elm Street away from him. The angle was easier now (17.4 degrees) and the limousine passed the obstruction of tree branches. Oswald's second bullet traveled 189 feet, hit President Kennedy in the upper back just to the right of the seventh vertebrae of his spinal column, and exited his neck tumbling toward Governor Connally. Connally was in the process of turning to his right. Before he completed his turn, he was hit in his back below his right armpit with the same bullet that hit President Kennedy. The bullet was retrieved on Connally's stretcher at Parkland Hospital.

Oswald reloaded again and quickly fired his third and final shot at a 15.2 degree angle five seconds later. The 265-foot shot hit President Kennedy in the back of the head. Bullet fragments found in the limousine and within President Kennedy's head were linked to Oswald's rifle. It is likely that a fragment from this shot found its way over Elm Street and hit the curb on Commerce Street to throw up concrete into James Tague's face. Oswald pulled the bolt action of his rifle again to load the fourth cartridge but did not fire.

Three Texas School Book Depository employees watching the motorcade from the fifth floor windows directly below Oswald's sniper's nest heard shots above them and the click of the bolt action to reload the rifle as well as shells hit the floor after their ejection from the rifle. The reverberation of the shots sent dust onto their heads. One of these men, Harold Norman, watched the motorcade from a fifth floor window directly beneath the sniper's nest. " . . . I heard three shots fired from, I believe, the floor above me . . . I heard a shot and several seconds later I heard two more shots. I knew that the shots had come from directly above me, and I could hear the expended cartridges fall to the floor. I could also hear the bolt-action rifle."

Howard Brennan sat on a short concrete wall that faced the Texas School Book Depository and watched the sixth floor window from the south side of the Houston and Elm Street intersection. "And this man, the same man I saw prior to the President's arrival, was in the window and taking aim for his last shot. After he fired the last, or the third shot, he didn't seem to be in a great rush, hurry. He seemed to pause for a moment to see if for sure he accomplished his purpose, and he brought back the gun to rest in upright position as though he was satisfied."

# About the Author

John S. Craig is the author of *Peculiar Liaisons in War, Espionage, and Terrorism in the Twentieth Century* (2005, Algora Press); *Mile High Cold and Other Stories* (2012, Lulu Press); *Heroes, Rogues, and Spies* (2014, Lulu Press); *The Guns of Dealey Plaza – Weapons and the Kennedy Assassination* (2016, Lulu Press); *The Ace and Queen of The Great War Spies* (2021, Blurb); *The Dirge of the Black Orchestra – Saving Germany from Nazism* (2021, Blurb Press); *Military Tactical Deception and the Courageous Strikes Against the Axis Powers -- Col. T.E. Lawrence, General Jimmy Doolittle, and General Knut Haukelid* (2021, Blurb Press)

## End Notes

[1] Apis is "Bee" in Greek and "Bull" in Egyptian. Most biographers cite Apis as meaning "Bull."

[2] "The Black Hand" is borrowed from an old terrorist organization in Italy of the same name, La Mano Negra, that specialized in extortion since 1750.

[3] The term "Balkans" is sometimes understood to include Romania, as well, although in fact Romania lies to the north of the Balkan Peninsula. Speaking a Latin-based language, worshipping primarily according to the Orthodox Church, and having fought the Ottoman Turks for centuries, it encapsulates the region's difficult history.

[4] Kaplan, Robert. *Balkan Ghosts, A Journey Through History*, St. Martins, New York, 1933, p. xviii.

[5] Nikola Tesla, a Serbian born July 9, 1856 in Croatia, became a US citizen and developed the alternating-current (AC) power system, the radio, fluorescent lights, and more than 100 US patents.

[6] The Oracle of Delphi dates back to 1400 BC and was the most important shrine in all Greece. It was considered the center of the earth

and was built around a sacred spring. The Pythia, an elderly priestess who interpreted the will of Apollo, answered questions concerning the future, which could include everything from farming schedules to matters of war. The vapors from a spring would put the Pythia into a trance where she would hear the words of Apollo. The gases emanating from the spring have been described as giving the Pythia a "narcotic" or "anesthetic" effect.

[7] Spartacus was a Thracian enslaved by the Romans. His slave uprising occurred in 73-71 BC and was known as the "Third Servile War." Thrace is an ancient area that covered northeastern Greece, southern Bulgaria, and parts of western Turkey, bordered by the Black Sea, the Aegean Sea, and the Sea of Marmara.

[8] Shea, John. *Macedonia and Greece — The Struggle to Define a New Balkan Nation*, McFarland, Jefferson, N.C., 1997, p. 26.

[9] Numerous conspiracy theories surround the death of Philip. One popular version is that Philip's lover, Pausanias, acted alone in stabbing Philip with a sword at the wedding ceremony of Philip's daughter.

[10] Dinocrates, Alexander's personal architect, designed Alexandria, Egypt. Legend says Alexandria contained a library and museum that

eventually held every great work of literature in the world. The library and museum flourished from roughly 300 BC to AD 300. Every great literary work of the Greeks was held there, as well as collections of Roman, Jewish, and Arabian scholarly works.

[11] Alexander was motivated and influenced by a politically savvy father; an ambitious mother who was interested in revenge, cults, and oracles; and the great Aristotle, who was hired by Philip to be Alexander's personal tutor. Alexander carried Aristotle's annotated copy of Homer's *The Iliad* on his conquests, believing that Homer's heroes embodied the epitome of courage and virtue ("This is the one best omen, to fight in defense of one's country . . . *The Iliad*, Book 9).

[12] Constantine I (also known as Constantine the Great, Flavius Valerius Constantinus, Roman Emperor from 312-337) passed the Edict of Milan (AD 313) that granted religious toleration of Christianity throughout the Roman Empire.

[13] Flavius Theodosius, Roman Emperor from 379-95, ensconced his sons in the two empires: Arcadius in the East and Honorius in the West.

[14] Serbia's history as a Balkan nation began in the middle seventh century. The Kingdom of Serbs, Croats, and Slovenes was formed in 1918. The name was changed to Yugoslavia in 1929. At

the end of the twentieth century Serbia was one of two republics making up the Federal Republic of Yugoslavia, Montenegro being the other.

[15] Muhammad's full name is Abu al-Qasim Muhammad ibn 'Abd Allah ibn Abd al-Muttalib ibn Hashim.

[16] Price, Randall. *Unholy War*, Harvest House Publishers, Eugene, Oregon, 2001, pp. 319-323.

[17] In 1054, Patriarch of Constantinople Michael Caerularius, refused to the give an audience to a group of the pope's delegates in Constantinople for three months. This affront eventually created mutual acts of ex-communication between the East and West that were not lifted until 1965.

[18] Armstrong, Karen. *Holy War*, Anchor, New York, 2001, p. 267.

[19] *Ibid.*, pp. 271-274. In 1204, Crusaders sacked Constantinople without the permission of the Pope. The Children's Crusade was undertaken in 1212 when a huge number of European children, with an average age of 12, were gathered up and sent on a march to the Holy Land. The Crusade ended within a year. Most of the young Crusaders died of hunger or were kidnapped and sold into slavery.

[20] Judah, Tim. *The Serbs: History, Myth and the Destruction of Yugoslavia,* New Haven, Yale University, 1998, p. 1.

[21] *Ibid.,* pp. 49-50.

[22] Glenny, Misha. *The Balkans, Nationalism, War and the Great Powers*, 1804-1999, Viking, New York, 2000, p. 126.

[23] Brook-Shepherd, Gordon. *Royal Sunset*, Doubleday and Co., Garden City, New York, 1987.

[24] Provinces in 1914 included Bohemia, Moravia, Bukovina, Transylvania, Carniola, Kustenland, Dalmatia, Croatia, Fiume, Bosnia-Hercegovina, and Galicia. The western portion of Austria-Hungary was also called Cisleithana, since it contained the portion of that monarchy on the near (that is, western) side of the river Leitha.

[25] Brook-Shepherd, Gordon. *Archduke of Sarajevo*, Little Brown Co., Boston/Toronto, 1984, p. 127.

[26] Cohen, Philip J. *Serbia's Secret War*, Texas A&M Press, College Station, Texas, 1996, p. 6.

[27] Kaplan, Robert. *Balkan Ghosts, A Journey Through History*, St. Martins, 1933, New York, pp. 52, 65.

[28] Mackenzie, David. *Apis: The Congenial Conspirator, The Life of Col. Dragutin Dimitrijevic*, East

European Monographs, Boulder, Colorado, Distributed by Columbia University Press, New York, 1989, p. 66.

[29] Brook-Shepherd, Gordon. *Archduke of Sarajevo*, Little Brown Co., Boston/Toronto, 1984, p. 219.

[30] Cassels, Lavender. *The Archduke and the Assassin*, Scarborough House, Briarcliff, New York, 1984.

[31] *Ibid.*, p. 229.

[32] Ivo Andric won the 1962 Nobel Prize for Literature as author of *The Bridge on the Drina* and *Bosnian Chronicle*.

[33] Glenny, Misha. *The Balkans, Nationalism, War and the Great Powers*, 1804-1999, Viking, New York, 2000, p. 302.

[34] Dedijer, Vladimir. *The Road to Sarajevo*, Simon Shuster, New York, 1966, p. 355.

[35] Tuchman, Barbara, *The Guns of August*, Macmillan, New York, 1962, p. 3.

[36] Glenny, Misha. *The Balkans, Nationalism, War and the Great Powers*, 1804-1999, Viking, New York, 2000, p. 284.

[37] Whitehouse, Arch. *Heroes and Legends of World War I*, Doubleday, Garden City, 1964, p. 4.

38 Ferdinand intended on replacing the Dual Monarchy with a three-part system, which would see the German and Czechs in the first part, Hungary the second, and the southern Slavs of Croatia, Dalmatia, Bosnia and Hercegovina the third part.

39 Mackenzie, David. *Apis: The Congenial Conspirator, The Life of Col. Dragutin Dimitrijevic*, East European Monographs, Boulder, Colorado, Distributed by Columbia University Press, New York, 1989, p.124-5.

40 Wallechinsky, David and Wallace, Irving. *The People's Almanac*, Doubleday, Garden City, N.J., p. 505.

41 Barnes, Harry Elmer. *The Genesis of the World War, An Introduction to the Problem of War Guilt*, Howard Fertig, New York, 1970, p. 161.

42 King, Greg. *The Assassination of the Archduke: Sarajevo 1914 and the Romance That Changed the World*, St. Martins, New York, 2013. "The fifty years preceding that golden summer of 1914 witnessed constant violence. Assassination was common: The sultan of Turkey was killed in 1876; American President James Garfield and Tsar Alexander II of Russia in 1881; President Sadi Carnot of France in 1894; the shah of Persia in 1896; the prime minister of Spain in 1897; the empress of Austria in 1898; King

Umberto of Italy in 1900; American President William McKinley in 1901; King Alexander and Queen Draga of Serbia in 1903; Grand Duke Sergei Alexandrovich of Russia in 1905; King Carlos of Portugal and his son Crown Prince Luis Felipe in 1908; Russian prime minister Peter Stolypin in 1911; and King George of Greece in 1913."

[43] Brook-Shepherd, Gordon. *Archduke of Sarajevo*, Little Brown Co., Boston/Toronto, 1984, p. 244.

[44] Cassels, Lavender. *The Archduke and the Assassin*, Scarborough House, Briarcliff, New York, 1984, p. 66.

[45] Pusara escaped into the crowd and was arrested hours later as he sang in a choir celebrating the Vidovdan holiday. Princip tried to clear Pusara of any guilt in the assassination. Kaplan, Robert. *Balkan Ghosts, A Journey Through History*, St. Martins, 1933, New York, p. 323.

[46] Dedijer, Vladimir. *The Road to Sarajevo*, Simon Shuster, New York, 1966, pp. 319-322.

[47] Devoss, David. "Searching for Gavrilo Princip," *Smithsonian*, August 2000, p. 42.

[48] Burg, David and Purcell, L. Edward. *Almanac of World War I*, University Press of Kentucky, Lexington, Kentucky, 1998, p. 11.

[49] Princip, by one account, was born on June 13, 1884 but a mistake in the official entry of his birth date by the delivering doctor made his official date of July 13, 1884, which made him under twenty at the time of the shooting and too young for capital punishment.

[50] Nedjelko Cabrinovic (who threw a bomb) was sentenced to 20 years and died of tuberculosis in prison in 1916. Vasco Cubrilovic (who was armed with a revolver, but was too afraid to shoot) was sentenced to 16 years and released by the Allies in 1918. Trifko Grabez was sentenced to 20 years. He died of tuberculosis in prison in 1916. Danilo Ilic was executed February 3, 1915. Mohammed Mehmedbasic returned to Sarajevo 1919 and was pardoned for his role in the assassination. Cvijetko Popovic (the motorcade lookout) was sentenced to 13 years.

[51] Koning, Hans. *Death of a School-Boy*, Harcourt, Brace, Jovanovich, New York, 1974.

[52] Gilbert, Martin. *A History of the Twentieth Century*, Harper Collins, 1977, New York, v. 1, pp. 316.

[53] Milan Ciganovic provided six Serbian Army issue hand grenades, four Browning pistols, ammunition, and vials of poison to the assassins.

[54] Gilbert, Martin. *A History of the Twentieth Century*, Harper Collins, 1977, New York, v. 1, p. 317.

[55] The novel and film presented a strong anti-war message. Initially rejected as unreadable, it became a phenomenal bestseller and was translated into 15 languages.

[56] Dedijer, Vladimir. *The Road to Sarajevo*, Simon Shuster, New York, 1966, p. 396.

[57] Mackenzie, David. *Apis: The Congenial Conspirator, The Life of Col. Dragutin Dimitrijevic*, East European Monographs, Boulder, Colorado, Distributed by Columbia University Press, New York, 1989, p.178.

[58] Brehm, Bruno. *They Call It Patriotism*, trans. Goldsmith, Margaret (Apis und Este), Little Brown, and Co., Boston, Massachusetts, 1932.

[59] On July 1, 1916, the first day of the battle of the Somme, more than 100,000 British and French soldiers formed three lines fifteen miles long, jumped from their trenches and slowly marched in columns into German machine guns firing at one hundred rounds per minute, a technical horror no army had ever faced. By the end of the day the British Army alone had 57,470 casualties, the biggest loss ever suffered by any army in a single day.

[60] Audoin-Rouzeau, Stephane, Becker, Annette. *14-18 Understanding the Great War*, Farrar, Straus, and Giroux, New York, 2002, pp. 21-47. In March of 1918 the Spanish influenza spread from soldiers at Fort Riley, Kansas to other military installations throughout the country and the world. It killed 21.6 million worldwide, 12.5 million in India alone. Wallechinsky, David and Wallace, Irving. *The People's Almanac*, Doubleday, Garden City, N.J., p. 547.

[61] Axelrod, Alan. *The Complete Idiot's Guide to World War I*, Alpha Books, Indianapolis, Indiana, 2000, p. 3.

[62] Stallings, Laurene. *The First World War — A Photo History*, Simon and Schuster, New York, 1933. The French lost nearly two million soldiers and the Germans a little over two million soldiers. Conservative estimates for deaths of Serbians were 775,000, which included soldiers and citizens that died due to disease and starvation — 15 percent of the Serbian population; the French lost 16% of their soldiers, the Germans 15.4 %, Serbia 37%, Turkey, 27%, Romania 25%, Bulgaria 22%.

[63] Balakian, Peter. *The Burning Tigris: The Armenian Genocide and America's Awakening to International Human Rights*, Harper Collins, New York, 2003.

[64] Gilbert, Martin. *A History of the Twentieth Century*, Harper Collins, 1977, New York, v. 1, p. 915.

[65] Robson, Stuart. *The First World War*, Longman, London/New York, 1995, pp. 1-2.

[66] *Ochrana* was the intelligence and secret service under the Russian czars from 1881 to 1917.

[67] Dedijer, Vladimir. *The Road to Sarajevo*, Simon Shuster, New York, 1966, p. 20.

[68] The Alexandria-Washington Lodge of Virginia defines Freemasonry as "the oldest and the largest fraternal order in the world. It is a universal brotherhood of men dedicated to serving God, family, fellowman and country. The heritage of modern Freemasonry is derived from the organized guilds or unions of stonemasons who constructed the beautiful cathedrals and other stately structures throughout Europe during the middle ages."

[69] Dedijer, Vladimir. *The Road to Sarajevo*, Simon Shuster, New York, 1966, p. 18.

[70] Kampschror, Beth. "The Assassin's Footsteps," *Transitions Online*, March 17, 2003.

[71] Kaplan, Robert. *Balkan Ghosts, A Journey Through History*, St. Martins, 1933, New York, pp.54-5.

[72] Gerolymatos, Andre. *The Balkan Wars — Conquest, Revolution, and Retribution from the Ottoman Era to the Twelfth Century and Beyond*, Basic Books, New York, 2002, p. 207.

[73] General Foch rose to command the French Ninth Army in the French counter-attack at Marne. Foch uttered his famous line in September 1914: "My center is giving way, my right is retreating, situation excellent, I am attacking."

[74] Keegan, John. *The First World War*, Knopf, New York, 1999, p. 4.

[75] Burg, David and Purcell, L. Edward. *Almanac of World War I*, University Press of Kentucky, Lexington, KY, 1998, p. 10.

[76] Audoin-Rouzeau, Stephane and Becker, Annette. *14-18 Understanding the Great War*, Farrar, Straus, and Giroux, New York, 2002, p. 1.

[77] Audoin-Rouzeau, Stephane, Becker, Annette. *14-18 Understanding the Great War*, Farrar, Straus, and Giroux, New York, 2002, p. 159.

[78] Gerolymatos, Andre. *The Balkan Wars — Conquest, Revolution, and Retribution from the Ottoman Era to the Twelfth Century and Beyond*, Basic Books, New York, 2002, p. 192.

[79] Sulzberger, C.L. *A Long Row of Candles — Memoirs and Diaries*, 1934-54, MacMillan Co., 1969, p. 64.

[80] Coogan, Tim Pat. *The Man Who Made Ireland*. Roberts Rinehart Publishing, Niwot, Colorado, 1992, p. 116.

[81] As the Nazi party gained in power and influence in the 1930s in Germany, the Irish Republican Army was also gaining ground in Ireland. IRA man Frank Ryan was trained as a saboteur in Berlin in May of 1940, though he never returned to Ireland to use his knowledge. *Abwehr* agents Herman Goetz and Ernst W. Drohl failed to create an alliance with the IRA, though the two made it to the shores of Ireland. Moloney, Ed. *A Secret History of the IRA*, W.W. Norton, New York, 2002, pp. 3-10.

[82] Currie, Stephen. *Terrorists and Terrorism Groups*, Lucent Books, San Diego, Ca., 2002, pp. 42-56.

[83] Huelsenbeck would declare in 1970 that the Dada movement was "against the war [and] all ideology, because the ideology based on Kant and Fichte and Hegel had become compatible with war... the culture of Goethe and Schiller had become compatible with war ... we were not politicians, we were artists, painters and poets ... we expressed ourselves in art, even though we

were against art. That is the basic paradox of Dadaism, which has not been resolved to this day." Friedrich, Otto. *Before the Deluge — A Portrait of Berlin in the 1920s*, Harper and Row, New York, 1972, pp. 37, 51, 148-9.

[84] Bulgarian assassin Vlada Cherozamsky (aka Georgiev) was on the run for a number of assassinations. He was hired by the IMRO and killed by French security guards immediately following the attack on Alexander.

[85] Pavelic and his hardliner Croatian nationalists, as well as the IMRO and Macedonian nationalists, were outraged over Alexander's hard Serbian rule of their lands. Believing that Alexander's suspension of the Yugoslavian constitution as well as his military dictator style of rule would keep Croatia from independence, Pavelic acted with the backing of Mussolini and the Hungarians in his quest to cripple the Serbian rule.

[86] John Fitzgerald Kennedy was the fourth American president to be victim of assassination, preceded by Abraham Lincoln in 1865 (Booth, a southern Democrat), James A. Garfield in 1881 (Cuiteau, a Republican), and William McKinley in 1901 (Czolgosz, an anarchist).

[87] WC, p. 110. "three shots were fired; it follows that one shot probably missed the car and

its occupants. The evidence is inconclusive as to whether it was the first, second, or third shot which missed."

[88] For a detailed analysis of the purchase of the rifle, see Martha Moyers article "Ordering the Rifle," *Assassination Chronicles*, v.2, n. 1, March 1996.

In March 1963, Lee Harvey Oswald, using the alias "A. Hidell," purchased by mail order a 6.5-millimeter Carcano Model 91/38 carbine, improperly called a Mannlicher–Carcano.

The Oswald rifle is an Italian Fucile di Fanteria (Eng: Infantry rifle) Modello 91/38 (Model 1891/1938) manufactured at the Royal Arms Factory in Terni, Italy, in 1940. The Model 91 bolt-action was manufactured and introduced in 1891 by Salvatore Carcano for the Turin Army Arsenal. After 1895, the Modello 91 used an *en bloc* ammunition clip similar to the Austrian Mannlicher ammunition clips, thus "Mannlicher" and "Carcano" came to be associated with Oswald's infamous rifle. The ammunition used in the clip was the 6.5 × 52 mm Cartuccia Modello 1895 rimless cartridge aka Mannlicher–Carcano ammunition.

Overall length when assembled: 40.12 inches (102.1 cm); longest piece when disassembled: 34.8 inches (88.4 cm).

Western Cartridge Co. ammunition with a 160 grain (10.37 g) round nose bullet. Side-mounted

Ordnance Optics 4 × 18 telescopic sight.
Warren Commission: "The bolt-action, clip-fed rifle found on the sixth floor of the Depository, described more fully in appendix X, is inscribed with various markings, including 'MADE ITALY,' 'CAL. 6.5,' '1940' and the number C2766.126 (See Commission Exhibit Nos. 1303, 541(2) and 541(3), pp. 82-83.) These markings have been explained as follows: 'MADE ITALY' refers to its origin; 'CAL. 6.5' refers to the rifle's caliber; '1940' refers to the year of manufacture; and the number C2766 is the serial number. This rifle is the only one of its type bearing that serial number.127 After review of standard reference works and the markings on the rifle, it was identified by the FBI as a 6.5-millimeter model 91/38 Mannlicher-Carcano rifle.128 Experts from the FBI made an independent determination of the caliber by inserting a Mannlicher-Carcano 6.5-millimeter cartridge into the weapon for fit, and by making a sulfur cast of the inside of the weapon's barrel and measuring the cast with a micrometer.129 From outward appearance, the weapon would appear to be a 7.35-millimeter rifle, but its mechanism had been rebarreled with a 6.5-millimeter barrel.130 Constable Deputy Sheriff Weitzman, who only saw the rifle at a glance and did not handle it, thought the weapon looked like a 7.65 Mauser bolt- action rifle.131 (See chapter V, p. 235.)"

[89] Goldberg, Robert A. *Enemies Within — The Culture of Conspiracy in Modern America*, Yale University Press, New Haven, Ct., 2001, pp. 105-149.

[90] Ephron, Nora. "The Assassination Reporters," *The Most of Nora Ephron*, Knopf, New York, 2013, pp. 17-21. For details concerning the number and names of photographers, both still and film, see Bugliosi, Vincent. *Reclaiming History: The Assassination of President John F. Kennedy*, W.W. Norton and Company, 2007, endnote 452. Other investigations of the assassination and related issues beyond the Warren Commission and the HSCA were done by the FBI, Secret Service, Dallas Police Department, Rockefeller Commission, Ramsey Clark Panel, and the Church Committee. Millions of tax dollars have been spent on these investigations. The HSCA supposedly spent 5 million dollars on their investigation.

[91] Thomas, D.B. "Echo correlation analysis and the acoustic evidence in the Kennedy assassination revisited," *Scientific and Justice*, v. 41, n. 1, 2001, pp. 21-32; HSCA Proceedings v. 8, p. 116; HSCA Final Report, p. 95.

[92] Getler, Warren and Brewer, Bob. *Shadow of the Sentinel*, Simon and Schuster, New York, 2003, pp. 15, 66-69. The Knights of the Golden Circle were a secret order of Southern sympathizers

throughout the north and south that plotted a resurrection of violence against the United States' Federal government.

[93] Jones, Howard. *Death of a Generation — How the Assassination of Diem and JFK Prolonged the Vietnam War*, Oxford University Press, Oxford, England, 2003, p. 1.

[94] O'Leary, Brad and Seymour, L.E. *Triangle of Death — The Shocking Truth About the Role of South Vietnam and the French Mafia in the Assassination of JFK*, WND Books, Nashville, Tennessee, 2003, p. 200.

[95] Mantik, David W. *Murder in Dealey Plaza*, "Paradoxes of the JFK Assassination: The Zapruder Film Controversy," ed. Fezter, James, Catfeet Press, Chicago, 2000, p. 325.

[96] Russo, Gus. *Live by the Sword*, Bancroft Press, Baltimore, 1998, pp. 87-88.

[97] Thornley describes the novel *The Idle Warriors* as a story that "centers around the gradual moral disintegration of a marine who, at last, defects to Russia." Thornley, Kerry W. *Oswald*, New Classics, Chicago, Il., 1965, p. 45.

[98] Russell, Dick. *The Man Who Knew Too Much*, Carroll and Graf, 1992, p. 218.

[99] Mahl, Tom. *Espionage's Most Wanted*, Brassey's, Washington, D.C., 2003, p. 86.

[100] Russell, Dick. *The Man Who Knew Too Much*, Carroll and Graf, 1992, p. 278.

[101] Hinckle, Warren and Turner, William. *Deadly Secrets — The CIA-Mafia War Against Castro and the JFK Assassination*, Thunder's Mouth Press, New York, 1992, p. 238.

[102] Aarons, Mark and Loftus, Jack. *The Secret War Against the Jews*, St. Martins, New York, 1994, p. 369.

[103] Hinckle, Warren and Turner, William. *Deadly Secrets — The CIA-Mafia War Against Castro and the JFK Assassination*, Thunder's Mouth Press, New York, 1992, p. 238.

[104] Russo, Gus. *Live by the Sword*, Bancroft Press, Baltimore, 1998, pp. 87-91.

[105] Russell, Dick. *The Man Who Knew Too Much*, Carroll and Graf, 1992, pp. 43-45.

[106] Kelin, John. "Richard Case Nagell: 1930-1995," *Fair Play*, Jan.-Feb. 1996. Jim Garrison investigators interviewed David Kroman, a prisoner of Leavenworth Penitentiary and an acquaintance of Richard Case Nagell. The investigators reported that Nagell told Kroman that a right-wing extremist group financed by H.L. Hunt and some Batista sympathizers had plotted to assassinate Kennedy in Dec. of 1962.

[107] Twyman, Noel. *Bloody Treason*, Laurel, Rancho Santa Fe, Ca., 1997, p. 607.

[108] *Ibid.*, pp. 612-3. Twyman provides a brief synopsis of "parallels" between Nagell and Oswald, such as a similar alias Hidell/Hidel; connections with the Fair Play for Cuba Committee in the US; owning miniature spy cameras; visiting Mexico City at the same time; having connections with the FBI and CIA and possible double agent status, to name just a few.

[109] *Ibid.*, p. 613. Alpha 66 carried out a series of attacks on Soviet ships in Cuban ports in March of 1963. JFK quickly disassociated himself and the government from the actions, which came on the heels of the Cuban missile crisis, though members of the group gave the impression in a Washington press conference that they had official backing.

[110] Russell, Dick. *The Man Who Knew Too Much*, Carroll and Graf, 1992, p. 699.

[111] Newman, John. *Oswald and the CIA*, Carroll and Graff, 1995, p. 104.

[112] Summers, Anthony, *Conspiracy*, Paragon, New York, 1989, pp. 504-6. See also Fonzi, Gaeton. *The Last Investigation*, Thunder's, 1993.

[113] Twyman, Noel. *Bloody Treason*, Laurel, Rancho Santa Fe, Ca., 1997, pp. 555-6. The letter

was sent to investigator Penn Jones, Jr. from Mexico City in August of 1975 with a note in Spanish saying that another copy had been sent to the FBI.

[114] Connally reported to President Johnson that Garrison believed Khrushchev and Kennedy made a deal after the 1962 missile crisis to allow Castro to stay in power. As the theory goes, six months later Robert Kennedy ordered the CIA to send assassination squads to Cuba to kill Castro but they failed and Castro sent four-man teams into the US to get JFK. In a March 2, 1967 conversation with Johnson, Governor Connally said: "Garrison has information that would prove that there were four assassination [teams] . . . assassins in the United States, sent here by [Fidel] Castro, or Castro's people. [Sent] not by Castro himself, but one of his lieutenants . . . One of the teams was composed of Lee Harvey Oswald; this fella [Clay] Shaw, that has just been arrested in New Orleans yesterday; and the [deceased] man [David] Ferrie; plus one other man. They were teams of four. And there were two other teams that I know nothing about." Connally gleaned much of this information from a WINS radio report in New York and a journalist, Paul Smith. Holland, Max. "The Assassination Tapes," *The Atlantic Monthly*, June 2004, p. 87.

[115] Robert Morrow's 1992 book *First Hand Knowledge* details several CIA missions in which Ferrie acted as a pilot for several of Morrow's covert operations in Cuba. Ferrie also served as an assistant to Morrow when he was instructed by the CIA to purchase weapons in Europe. Morrow candidly declares that Ferrie was the "brains" behind Shaw and Marcello's various operations, and that Ferrie was the central planner of the assassination.

[116] HSCA v. X, p. 394.

[117] *Ibid.*, p. 109.

[118] JFK document 014904.

[119] HSCA Report, Section IC3.

[120] Groups investigated by the HSCA included Alpha 66, the Cuban Revolutionary Junta (JURE), Commandos L, the Directorio Revolucionario Estudiantil (DRE), the Cuban Revolutionary Junta (JURE), the Cuban Revolutionary Council (CRC) which included the Frente Revolucinario Democratico (FRD), the Junta del Gobiemo de Cuba en el Exilio (JGCE), the 30th of November, the International Penetration Forces (InterPen), the Revolutionary Recovery Movement (MRR), and the Ejercito Invasor Cubano (EIC).

[121] The HSCA reported that the FAA, vo. 5 Attachment QQ document listed the submarines as being found "in Ferrie's house."

[122] FBI 62-109060-4344, 62-109060-4535; CIA 1363-501.

[123] Smith asked Eastern Airlines to give Ferrie a leave with pay for full-time work for the CRC. The request was denied, but Ferrie's vacation in April 1961 coincided with the Bay of Pigs invasion. HSCA v. X, p. 109. The HSCA was unable to find out whether Ferrie had any role in the invasion.

[124] HSCA v. X, p. 109.

[125] Interview with Layten Martens by Gus Russo. Gus Russo, *Live by the Sword*, Bancroft Press, Baltimore, 1998, p. 330

[126] *Ibid.*, p. 330.

[127] Weberman and Canfield. *Coup d'etat in America*, Quick American Archives, 1992, p. 36.

[128] November in Dallas Conference, November 23, 1996, The Hemming Panel.

[129] HSCA v. XIII, p. 491.

[130] Deposition of Adrian T. Alba, May 5, 1978, HSCA p. 19 (JFK Document 0099641).

[131] James, Rosemary and Wardlaw, Jack. *Plot or Politics?*, Pelican Publ., 1967, p. 49.

132 HSCA v. XIII, p. 466.

133 Roger Peterson. "Declassified," *American History*, July 1, 1996, p. 54.

134 According to Roberts, Banister told her directly that Oswald was working with their office. This information was obtained by Summers only when he paid her for an interview related to a television documentary. Roberts told Gerald Posner, author of *Case Closed*, that she didn't tell Summers "all the truth."

135 HSCA 180-10090-10315.

136 Furiati, Claudia. *ZR Rifle — The Plot to Kill Kennedy and Castro*, Ocean, 1994, pp. 148-9.

137 Scott, Peter Dale. *Deep Politics and the Death of JFK*. Berkeley and L.A., University of California Press, 1993. On the day Oswald handed out pro-Castro leaflets in New Orleans with the address of 544 Camp St. printed on them, Ferrie was leading an anti-Castro demonstration a few blocks away.

138 CE 3119, p. 771, Secret Service report 00-2-34,030. Voebel also claimed, with no additional substantiation, that he spotted Ferrie on television in a Dallas crowd only hours after the assassination in Dallas. Joesten, Joachim. *The Garrison Inquiry: Truth or Consquences,* Dawnay, London, 1967.

[139] Groden, Robert. *The Search for Lee Harvey Oswald*, Penguin Studio, 1995, p. 76.

[140] FBI file # 89-69.

[141] In 1954 Oswald joined the Civil Air Patrol. In an interview with *Look* magazine in 1967, Oswald's brother Robert told a reporter, "According to Lee's own later statement, 1954 was the year when he first became interested in communism . . . I can't help wondering whether it might have been Ferrie who introduced Lee to communist ideas. I realize that I have nothing solid on which to base such a speculation, except the timing."

[142] Martin's claim that Ferrie was in Texas was found to be false. Ferrie's Stinson Voyager airplane was found to be inoperable. An FAA document showed that Martin believed that Ferrie's airplane was airworthy as of July 1963, or that Ferrie had access to a Stinson. Martin retracted his allegations concerning Ferrie in a statement to the Secret Service. HSCA v. X, p. 115.

[143] HSCA v. XII, p. 456.

[144] Canal, John. *Silencing the Lone Assassination*, Paragon, St. Paul, MN, 2001, p. 93.

[145] HSCA v. XII, p. 451.

[146] *Ibid.*, p. 455.

[147] Garrison believed the ice rink acted as a message center for Ferrie; his objective at the ice rink has never been revealed. However, Al Beauboeuf, a former roller skating champion, that investing in an ice skating rink could be profitable. For three weeks before the assassination, they had discussed the trip. Beauboeuf passed a lie detector on this issue in May of 1967. James, Rosemary and Ward, Jack. *Plot or Politics*, Pelican Publishing, 1967, p. 44.

[148] Twyman, Noel. *Bloody Treason*, Laurel, 1997, p. 275.

[149] Investigator Mike Sylwester suggests that framing Ferrie would implicate Marcello, an act that would only benefit other possible conspirators. The FBI questioned Gill about how he learned that Ferrie's card had been found in Oswald's wallet, but Gill replied that he could not recall who told him the "rumor." "*The Kennedy Contract*: A Review," *The Fourth Decade*, November 1993, v. 1 no. 1, p. 25. Davis, John H. *The Kennedy Contract*, McGraw Hill, 1992, pp. 113-114.

[150] Secret Service report 12-13-63, New Orleans Office, Agent Anthony Gerrets, Warren Commission Document 87.

[151] Reitzes, David. "Who is 'Willie O'Keefe'?," http://www.jfk-online.com/jfk100okeefe.html

[152] In a twist of this account, the previously mentioned Torbitt document (*Nomenclature of an Assassination Cabal*) has Ferrie and gunrunner Ray McKeown meeting Dallas detective Joe Cody in Houston. Cody had flown the conspirators, which included a grassy knoll gunman, to Houston. Ferrie then flew the conspirators to Matamoros, Mexico. Like Broshears's claims, this account is completely undocumented by any other source. Torbitt names Ferrie as a main player in Permindex.

[153] Interview with Perry Raymond Russo at the Mercy Hospital on February 27, 1967 by Andrew Sciambra.

[154] HSCA, Outside Contact Report, July 6, 1978. A March 1967 FBI report cited Jim Garrison's investigation that "a group of Cuban refugees training near Lake Pontchartrain, Louisiana, presumably during the period Oswald resided in New Orleans . . . these Cubans reportedly had been 'left in the lurch' and had become angry at everyone . . . some of these Cubans attended a meeting in the apartment of David William Ferrie. One of the Cubans was named Diaz . . . also present at the meeting were Clay Bertrand, aka Clay Shaw . . ." FBI report 62-109060.

[155] Groden, Robert. *The Search for Lee Harvey Oswald*, Penguin Studio, 1995, p. 18.

156 HSCA, JFK Record Number 157-10005-10276.

157 Posner, Gerald. "Garrison Guilty, Another Case Closed," *New York Times*, August 6, 1995. As ludicrous as this sounds, Bundy survived cross-examination from Shaw's attorney Irvin Dymond. Several members of the Garrison camp did not want Bundy to testify, but Garrison insisted.

158 HSCA, RG 233.

159 Kirkwood, James. *American Grotesque*, Harper, 1968, p. 175.

160 Fonzi, Gaeton. *The Last Investigation*, Thunder's, 1993, pp. 239, 375. Richard Helms, CIA director in 1967, wrote in his 2003 autobiography that from 1948 to 1956 Shaw offered information to the Domestic Contacts Service (DCS), a division of the CIA. The DCS offered no compensation for information from informants and took only voluntary information from American travelers, usually businessmen.

161 Russo, Gus. *Live By the Sword*, Bancroft Press, Baltimore, p. 411.

162 WC v. IX, p. 317.

163 Russell, Dick. *The Man Who Knew Too Much*, Carroll and Graf, New York, 2003, revised edition, pp. 206-7.

[164] Posner, Gerald. *Case Closed*, Random House, New York, 1993, p. 120.

[165] Turner, K.S. "From April To November and Back Again," *The Third Decade* v. 8, n. 1, pp. 1-5, November 1991.

[166] Kelly, William E. "A New Oswald Witness Goes Public," September, 1999. http://www.pir.org/edisen.html.

[167] HSCA v. XII, p. 401.

[168] Haslam, Edward T. *Mary, Ferrie, and the Monkey Virus*, Wordsworth, 1995.

[169] HSCA v. X, p. 112.

[170] Marcello employed Oswald's uncle Charles Murret as a bookmaker in the New Orleans gambling world. In the 1970s the FBI wiretapped many of Marcello's phone conversations. However, the FBI has refused to release 161 reels of tape containing these conversations. An FBI informant, Joe Hauser, who claimed he made several of these recordings, told author John H. Davis that Marcello spoke of involvement in the assassination and that he personally knew Oswald.

[171] HSCA v. XII, p. 442.

[172] Whitmey, Peter R. "Did David Ferrie Lie to the Secret Service?" *The Fourth Decade*, January 1996, v. 3, no. 2, pp. 5-9.

[173] On November 26, 1963 a Georgian businessman, Gene Summer, told the FBI that he was sure he saw Oswald accept money from a man he believed was the owner of the Town and Country restaurant in Louisiana.

[174] O'Leary, Brad and Seymour, L.E. *Triangle of Death — The Shocking Truth About the Role of South Vietnam and the French Mafia in the Assassination of JFK*, WND Books, Nashville, Tennessee, 2003, p. 179.

[175] Whitmey, Peter R. "The Winnipeg Airport Incidents," *The Fourth Decade*, November 1995, v.3 no. 1, p. 23.

[176] *Ibid.*

[177] Russell, Dick. *The Man Who Knew Too Much*, Carroll and Graf, 1992, pp. 120-1.

[178] Torbitt, William. *Nomenclature of an Assassination Cabal*, www.parapscope.com/articles/1196/torbitt.htm

[179] On March 4, 1967, three days after Clay Shaw was arrested for complicity in the assassination of JFK, an Italian newspaper with strong communist ties, *Il Paese Sera,* reported that Clay Shaw was one of the directors of the Rome World Trade Centre, an organization that was run by the CIA to undermine communism. The CIA had admitted that Shaw was a contact for the

agency's Domestic Contact Service during the 1950s. *Il Paese Sera* had strong links to Italian Fascists and Permindex (Permanent Industrial Exhibitions). Dorrill, Steve. "Permindex: The International Trade in Disinformation," *The Third Decade*, v.2, no. 1, November 1985, pp. 11-15. Permindex is mentioned extensively in the Torbitt document, which has been called one of the most important "underground" documents in assassination literature filled with a dizzying array of conspirators, secret societies, government agencies, and business conglomerations. In Torbitt's version of the assassination the planning and supervision came from Division Five of the FBI, a supposedly small department focusing on espionage and counter-espionage, developed with the blessing of Hoover and run by his associate William Sullivan. CIA contract agent Robert Morrow claimed that while working at Permindex in the early sixties he received a call from David Ferrie from Switzerland.

[180] To remove any doubt about the credibility of this work, it has been published under the title of *NASA, Nazis and JFK — The Torbitt document and the JFK Assassination*, a book that "links Area 51, *Operation Paperclip*, NASA, JFK and others . . ."

[181] Whitmey, Peter R. "The Winnipeg Airport Incidents," *The Fourth Decade*, November 1995, v.3 no. 1, pp. 24-25.

[182] Russell, Dick. *The Man Who Knew Too Much*, Carroll and Graf, New York, 2003, revised edition, pp. 266-8.

[183] Thornley, Kerry. *The Idle Warriors*, Illuminet Press, Avondale Estates, Ga., 1991, pp. vii — viii.

[184] Peterson, Roger S. "Declassified," *American History*, July 1, 1996, p. 54.

[185] A CIA colleague told executive Assistant to the Deputy Director of the CIA Victor Marchetti that "Ferrie had been a contract agent to the Agency in the early sixties and had been involved in some of the Cuban activities." Marchetti was convinced that Ferrie was a CIA contract officer and involved in various criminal activities. Marchetti told author Anthony Summers "he observed consternation on the part of then CIA Director Richard Helms and other senior officials when Ferrie's name was first publicly linked with the assassination in 1967."

[186] On the day of Ferrie's death, Eladio del Valle was bludgeoned and shot to death by unknown assailants. Del Valle was an ex-city councilman from Havana during the Batista regime and worked in military intelligence. He was associated with Florida Mafia boss Santos Trafficante. Del Valle and Ferrie were members of

the Cuban Democratic Revolutionary Front, an organization devoted to overthrowing Castro.

[187] Garrison never publicly recognized any Mafia presence in New Orleans. Authors John H. Davis, Philip Melanson, attorney Frank Ragano, and Victor Marchetti, mercenary Gerry Hemming and many investigators have stated that Garrison's investigation was designed to protect Carlos Marcello from being linked to the assassination.

[188] HSCA Report, Section IC3, "Anti-Castro Cuban Groups may have been Involved."

[189] Mailer, Norman. *Oswald's Tale — An American Mystery*, Random House, 1995, p. 620.

[190] Moss, Armand. *Disinformation, Misinformation, and the "Conspiracy" to Kill JFK Exposed*, Archon, Armand, Conn., 1987, p. 116.

[191] HSCA p. IV, p. 483.

[192] The Minox may have been owned by Oswald or by his friends, the Paines, at whose house he was staying. Hewett, Caroll. "The Paines' Participation in the Minox Camera Charade," *Probe*, Nov.-Dec., 1996 v. 4, n. 1. Michael Griffith reports that the Minox camera had a serial number that did not exist among any Minox cameras sold within the US, suggesting that either the Paines or Oswald obtained the camera from outside the U.S. Griffith, Michael. "Just The Facts: Established

Facts about the JFK Assassination that Point to Conspiracy," 1998.

[193] Marrs, Jim. *Crossfire*, Carroll and Graf, New York, 1989, p. 186. Irvin Dymond, the New Orleans defense attorney representing Shaw in 1967, told Posner that the Clinton testimony was a "pack of lies. What the motive of the Clinton witnesses is I do not know, but it is clearly and demonstrably false." HSCA investigator, Gaeton Fonzi, wrote that the HSCA "found several very credible witnesses who saw Oswald during August 21-September 17 in Clinton, La. with Ferrie," and though the HSCA could not determine what Oswald was doing in Clinton "there was no doubt he was there." Fonzi, Gaeton. *The Last Investigation*, New York, Thunder's Mouth, 1993, pp. 240-241.

[194] The Minutemen in the 1960s were a clandestine combat militia headed by Robert DePugh, which held daily drills for its 25,000 members. The drills consisted of weapons training and guerilla warfare tactics under the motto of "Action Now" and the call for the "assassination of dangerous Communists." Hepburn, James. *Farewell America — The Plot to Kill JFK*, Penmarin Books, 2002, New York, 2003.

[195] Holden, William. "New Evidence Regarding Oswald's Activities in Clinton, Louisiana," *The Fourth Decade*, November 1996, v. 4, no. 1, pp. 5 - 18.

[196] *Ibid.*, p. 11.

[197] *Ibid.*, p. 18.

[198] CE 2286. Author William Holden reports that a Garrison employee, Tom Bethel, determined that the phone number was Welch's.

[199] Russo, Gus, *Live by the Sword*, Bancroft Press, Baltimore, 1998, p. 187.

[200] Canal, John. *Silencing the Lone Assassination*, Paragon, St. Paul, MN, 2001, p. 89. Canal asserts that Ruby may have received this money from either a down payment to hit Oswald or from his share of a gun smuggling operation at a National Guard Armory in Terrell, Texas on November 19, 1963. Gun smuggler Robert McKeown testified in front of the HSCA that he had been contacted by Ruby for a letter of introduction to Castro. McKeown also claims a visit from Oswald and a man named Hernandez who looking for Savage automatic rifles. Dallas attorney Carl Jarnagin wrote a letter to the FBI November 23, 1963 claiming he overheard a conversation between Ruby and Oswald concerning a hit on Governor John Connally in October of 1963. Hinckle, Warren and Turner, William. *Deadly Secrets — The CIA-Mafia War Against Castro and the JFK Assassination*, Thunder's Mouth Press, New York, 1992, p. 245.

[201] FBI report in National Archives number 180-10123-10039.

[202] Russell, Dick. *The Man Who Knew Too Much*, Carroll and Graf, 1992, pp. 706-7.

[203] Whitmey, Peter R. "The Winnipeg Airport Incidents," *The Fourth Decade*, November 1995, v.3 no. 1, p. 23.

[204] Whitmey, Peter. "Did Ferrie Lie to the F.B.I," *The Fourth Decade*, v. 3, n. 2, p.8.

[205] Reitzes, Dave. "Phone Factoid: Tortured Connection, http://mcadamsn.posc.mu.edu/factoid.htm

[206] WC v. 14, p. 58.

[207] An unidentified woman appeared in the Zapruder film wearing a scarf on her head and so was referred to as the Babushka Lady. Supposedly, federal authorities were unable to locate her for interviews for the Warren Commission. Beverly Oliver, an employee of Jack Ruby, was later mistakenly identified as the "Babushka Lady."

[208] Baker's claims include Oswald's affiliation with Dr. Mary Sherman, Clay Shaw, Ferrie, Guy Banister, plots to kill Castro with injected cancer, Jack Ruby, infiltration of anti-Kennedy assassination teams, David Atlee Phillips, Bobby Baker, and Billy Sol Estes. *The Men Who Killed*

*Kennedy*, "The Love Affair," (Nigel Turner Production, 2003).

[209] CE 2038.

[210] Noyes, Peter. *Legacy of Doubt*, Pinnacle Books, New York, 1973, pp. 117-118.

[211] Russell, Dick. *The Man Who Knew Too Much*, Carroll and Graf, 1992, p. 671.

[212] WC v. 5, p. 105.

[213] On March 30, 1961, Oswald was admitted to the Third Clinical Hospital's Ear, Nose, and Throat Division in Minsk for an adenoid operation. Author Lincoln Lawrence (a pseudonym) advances the fantastic theory in *Were We Controlled* that Oswald was implanted with a miniaturized radio receiver "which would produce a muscular reaction in his cerebral region." Russell, Dick. *The Man Who Knew Too Much*, Carroll and Graf, 1992, p. 675. Lawrence, Lincoln. *Were We Controlled*, University Books, New Hyde Park, New York, 1967.

[214] Russell, Dick. *The Man Who Knew Too Much*, Carroll and Graf, 1992, pp. 678-9.

[215] Mylroie, Laurie. *Study of Revenge: The First World Trade Center Attack and Saddam Hussein's War Against America*, AEI Press, Washington, D.C., 2001, p. 189 cited in Government's Memorandum of Law in Opposition to Defendant's PreTrial

Motions (Phase 1), p. 30, US v. Omar Abdul Rahman, et al. Omar's comment was allegedly made to one of Omar's follower's in 1993 when the follower was too hasty in his eagerness to bomb the U.N., a US Federal building, and the World Trade Center.

[216] Luken, John. *Oswald's Trigger Films — The Manchurian Candidate, We Were Strangers, Suddenly,* Falcon Books, Ann Arbor, Michigan, 2000.

[217] Rivele, Stephen J. *Kennedy: la conspiracion de la Mafia,* Ediciones, Barcelona, Spain, 1988.

[218] O'Leary Brad and Seymour L.E. *Triangle of Death — The Shocking Truth About the Role of South Vietnam and the French Mafia in the Assassination of JFK,* WND Books, Nashville, Tennessee, 2003, p. 192 (CIA doc # 632-796).

[219] Interview with KGB Colonel Ilya S. Pavlotsy, on video *The Secret KGB/JFK Assassination Fil*es, Associated Television, 1998, cited in O'Leary Brad and Seymour L.E. *Triangle of Death — The Shocking Truth About the Role of South Vietnam and the French Mafia in the Assassination of JFK*, WND Books, Nashville, Tennessee, 2003, p. 155.

[220] Hepburn, James. *Farewell America — The Plot to Kill JFK,* Penmarin Books, 2002, New York, 2003, p. 321. (Originally published as *L'Amerique Brule*).

[221] "David Ferrie's experience with the underground activities of the Cuban exile movement and as a private investigator for Carlos Marcello and Guy Banister might have made him a good candidate to participate in a conspiracy plot. He may not have known what was to be the outcome of his actions, but once the assassination had been successfully completed and his own name cleared, Ferrie would have had no reason to reveal his knowledge of the plot. Further, fear for his life may have prevented him from doing so." HSCA, v. X, p. 515.

[222] WC p. 124. "Fibers on Rifle. In a crevice between the butt plate of the rifle and the wooden stock was a tuft of several cotton fibers of dark blue, gray-black, and orange-yellow shades.64 On November 23, 1963, these fibers were examined by Paul M. Stombaugh, a special agent assigned to the Hair and Fiber Unit of the FBI Laboratory.65 He compared them with the fibers found in the shirt which Oswald was wearing when arrested in the Texas Theatre.66 This shirt was also composed of dark blue, gray-black and orange-yellow cotton fibers. Stombaugh testified that the colors, shades, and twist of the fibers found in the tuft on the rifle matched those in Oswald's shirt.67"

[223] Interview of Vincent Bugliosi with Robin Lindley, History News Network, Columbian College for Arts and Sciences, George Washington University, 2005.

[224] Litwin, Fred. "A Conspiracy Too Big? Intellectual Dishonesty in the JFK Assassination," 1994, Mcadmans.posc.mu.edu. Litwin points out that conspiracy theorists continue to investigate the possibility of the destruction, planting, tampering or forgery of evidence, as well as the issues of altering the body before autopsy, Oswald impersonators, police complicity, multiple assassins, and the supposed murder of scores of witnesses by unknown conspirators.

Litwin end note 107. "Paul Hoch has one of the more plausible theories about the assassination. 'One possibility - ironically - is that Oswald did it alone but so many people had things to cover up that the reaction of the government made it look like the assassination resulted from a conspiracy' (*Echoes of Conspiracy*, 3 November, 1993, pp.7). One could easily see the CIA not wanting to help an investigation that could possibly lead to exposure of its plots against Castro with the Mafia. Similarly, the FBI and Secret Service quite possibly wanted to cover some their tracks as well."

Litwin, Fred. "A Conspiracy Too Big? Intellectual Dishonesty in the JFK Assassination," 1994,

Mcadams.posc.mu.edu. "The HSCA addressed many of the issues raised by the critics in the sixties. Since then, the literature has taken on a disturbing tone – one that rejects any piece of evidence contrary to findings of conspiracy.[4] If the autopsy X-rays and photos show evidence of a single head- shot from the rear, well, they must be fakes. [5] If the wounds on Kennedy's body are consistent with a single-gunman, well, the body must have been altered. [6] If the neutron activation analysis shows the single-bullet theory to be correct, well, the evidence has been tampered with. [7] And, if you do not like the conclusions of a professional panel, well, they must have ties to the government. [8] One could go on and on. This is extremely dangerous. This development is exactly opposite to the legitimate process of theory-building and testing. In the clash between evidence and theories, theories have to be discarded. It's true that evidence is often weak and open to multiple interpretations, but to argue that evidence is fraudulent is to undermine the possibility that any theory might turn out to be 'true'. . . To argue in such a style is to cause the collapse of the entire empirical edifice of 'assassinology.' However weak, evidence could at least refute theories; now the evidence can't even do that.[9]"

[225] Bugliosi, Vincent. *Reclaiming History: The Assassination of President John F. Kennedy*, W.W.

Norton and Company, 2007. Sturdivan, Larry M., *The JFK Myths: A Scientific Investigation of the Kennedy Assassination*, Paragon House, 2005. Holland, Max. "The Truth was Out There," *Newsweek*, New York, 11/28/2014. Posner, Gerald. *Case Closed*, Random House, 1993. Cold Case JFK, Nova, PBS, November 2013. Sneed, Larry. *No More Silence*, Three Forks, Dallas, 1997. Craig, John S. *The Guns of Dealey Plaza — Weapons and the Kennedy Assassination*, LuLu, 2016.

[226] The following affidavit was executed by James Anthony Botelho on June 3, 1964 for the President's Commission on the Assassination of John F. Kennedy. Botelho was a roommate with Oswald while in the Marines. "Oswald once mentioned to me that he would like to go to Cuba to train Castro's troops because of the money he would earn."

[227] 1 H 23, 44; 2 HSCA, pp. 256–257.

[228] Bugliosi, Vincent, *Reclaiming History: The Assassination of President John F. Kennedy*, W.W. Norton and Company, 2007, p. 692.

[229] CE 2123; 24 H 665. Oswald left New Orleans September 24 or 25, 1963 for Mexico City hoping to get a transit visa to Cuba.

[230] Gus Russo's 1998 book *Live by the Sword: The Secret War against Castro and the Death of JFK* presents a case for Oswald as a lone gunman who

overtly threatened JFK in Mexico City just weeks before the assassination. Russo writes that Oswald, frustrated by being refused a visa by the Cubans at the Mexico City Embassy, screamed that he would kill Kennedy himself. Confirmation of a threat to Kennedy by Oswald came from various sources including Fidel Castro himself. Castro allegedly told British writer Comer Clark in July 1967 that Oswald wanted to work for the Cubans and had uncovered a CIA plot to kill Castro. "He said he wanted to 'free Cuba from American imperialism,' said Castro. Oswald's exact words were 'I'm going to kill that bastard. I'm going to kill Kennedy.' Castro said he was told of the remarks immediately but considered them a 'madman's ranting and not an offer.'" [Russo, Gus. *Live By the Sword*, Bancroft Press, Baltimore, 1998, pp. 223-4.] Within an interview of Castro by the HSCA, *he denied the Clark interview ever happened. Whether Oswald made these comments may never be known unless a recording can be produced or other reliable witnesses can be found to confirm Oswald's alleged and damning rant.*

[231] Bugliosi, Vincent. *Reclaiming History*, Norton and Co., New York, 2007, endnote 1286. "Though the evidence is clear that Oswald made no threat to kill Kennedy, as we have seen, the informant, Jack Childs, was indeed a very reliable source, and I believe he merely passed on to the FBI what Castro told him in Havana about the

threat. It was Castro who most likely was repeating information about the threat that he had received from his employees at the Cuban embassy, who in turn were merely passing on what an eventually discredited witness, Gilberto Alvarado Ugarte, said *he heard Oswald say outside the Cuban embassy.*"

[232] Latell, Brian. *Castro's Secrets: The CIA and Cuba's Intelligence Machine*, Palgrave Macmillan, 2012. Latell proposes in his book that Castro knew of Oswald's threats to assassinate President Kennedy but provides no proof. Though Kennedy's death would do nothing more than cast a suspicious eye on Castro, it is likely he met the news with dismay. In fact, he was with journalists at the time when he heard the news of the assassination. Castro was shocked saying, "*Es una mala noticia*" (this is bad news) according to Jean Daniel who was with him when he was informed of the assassination. Daniel, Jean. "When Castro Heard the News," *The New Republic*, December 7, 1963.

John McAdams: Review of Brian Latell's *Castro's Secrets: The CIA and Cuba's Intelligence Machine* (Palgrave Macmillan, 2012). *History News Network*, May 11, 2012. http://www.historynewsnetwork.org/article/1462 17 "Latell . . . argues that Castro himself micro-managed a lot of Cuban intelligence, and might have known about the confrontation at the embassy. He then argues that Oswald threatened Kennedy's life when leaving the embassy frustrated saying, 'I'm going to kill Kennedy for this.' Then he further asserts that Castro and Cuban intelligence actually knew that Oswald was going to shoot Kennedy about noon on November 22. What is the evidence on this? Latell posits -- *with absolutely no evidence* -- that Oswald had some contact with DGI [Cuba's foreign intelligence service, Directorio General de Inteligencia] officers in the Cuban embassy, and these would be people beyond the three individuals (two consuls and a secretary) with whom he is known to have interacted."

CPSIA information can be obtained
at www.ICGtesting.com
Printed in the USA
LVHW050726181121
703571LV00017B/877